Praise for *It's Momplicated*

I'm not sure I've read a more helpful book on how we daughters are shaped by our mothers' love—or unlove—as well as what to do about it. What am I sure about? In these pages you will find hope as well.

ELISA MORGAN
Speaker and author of *The Prayer Coin* and *The Beauty of Broken*

If your relationship with your mother is complex, problematic, difficult, and full of twists and turns, don't miss this book! Debbie Alsdorf and Joan Edwards Kay have combined their stories and their wisdom to help you understand the past, identify thorny issues, and lead you to right choices that will bring understanding, healing, and a deeper connection with God. This is a must-read book and is an important resource for individuals, counselors, and Christian leaders. I highly recommend *It's Momplicated*!

CAROL KENT
Speaker and author of *He Holds My Hand*

"Shouldn't this be easier?" That is the big question when it comes to mother-daughter relationships. But being both a mother and a daughter, I've realized that maybe it should be easier, but it just isn't. *It's Momplicated* has given me not only keen new insight into my own unmet needs, but compassion for a loving mom who tried to meet my spoken—and unspoken—needs. Another great benefit of reading Debbie and Joan's excellent book is the insight it's given me into understanding and connecting with my adult daughter in the ways that she needs a mom and always will. A healing and, most of all, freeing read. Highly recommended.

KATHI LIPP
Speaker and bestselling author of *The Husband Project* and *Clutter Free*

It's Momplicated is a skillful, well-laid-out blend of the spiritual, emotional, and psychological aspects to understanding the influence of this primary relationship between moms and daughters. It provides a respectful, substantial structure for exploration of both the gifts and the pain of this relationship and charts an informed course for healing and celebration. As a mom and daughter, I found it personally and profoundly transformative in one reading, but I know I will revisit it time and time again. As a clinician, I can see this being a great therapeutic intervention for those struggling to have healthy relationships. This is not just a book for moms and daughters, but for anyone wanting to understand how our earliest relationships are impacting how we relate to others now, offering a way to remove the obstacles that often prevent relationships from being all they can be.

MARY JEAN WALTON, MA, LMFT
Executive director of the Christian Counseling Center, San Jose, California

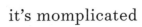

it's momplicated

it's momplicated

Hope and healing
for imperfect daughters
of imperfect mothers

Debbie Alsdorf | **Joan Edwards Kay,** MA, LMFT

TYNDALE
MOMENTUM®

*The nonfiction imprint of
Tyndale House Publishers, Inc.*

Visit Tyndale online at www.tyndale.com.

Visit Tyndale Momentum online at www.tyndalemomentum.com.

TYNDALE, Tyndale Momentum, and Tyndale's quill logo are registered trademarks of Tyndale House Publishers, Inc. The Tyndale Momentum logo is a trademark of Tyndale House Publishers, Inc. Tyndale Momentum is the nonfiction imprint of Tyndale House Publishers, Inc., Carol Stream, Illinois.

It's Momplicated: Hope and Healing for Imperfect Daughters of Imperfect Mothers

Designed by Julie Chen

Edited by Bonne Steffen

Published in association with the literary agency of Books & Such Literary Management, 52 Mission Circle, Suite 122, PMB 170, Santa Rosa, CA 95409.

All stories in this book, unless otherwise noted, are composites. Names and details have been changed to protect confidentiality.

For information about special discounts for bulk purchases, please contact Tyndale House Publishers at csresponse@tyndale.com, or call 1-800-323-9400.

Library of Congress Cataloging-in-Publication Data
Names: Alsdorf, Debbie, author.
Title: It's momplicated : hope and healing for imperfect daughters of imperfect mothers / Debbie Alsdorf, Joan Edwards Kay, MA, LMFT.
Description: Carol Stream, Illinois : Tyndale House Publishers, Inc., 2018. | Includes bibliographical references.
Identifiers: LCCN 2018017670 | ISBN 9781496435903 (hc : alk. paper) | ISBN 9781496426574 (sc : alk. paper)
Subjects: LCSH: Mothers and daughters—Religious aspects—Christianity. | Mothers and daughters. | Mothers—Religious life. | Daughters—Religious life.
Classification: LCC BV4529.18 .A54 2018 | DDC 248.8/431—dc23 LC record available at https://lccn .loc.gov/2018017670

Printed in the United States of America

24	23	22	21	20	19	18
7	6	5	4	3	2	1

To my sister, Sharon. You were a light in my childhood, and I will always thank God for you. I am stronger because of your love.

Debbie

∿

To Sara and Juli, who love me despite my momplicated ways. You are my greatest legacy.

Joan

table of contents

Even if my father and mother abandon me,
the LORD will hold me close.

PSALM 27:10

Can a mother forget her nursing child?
Can she feel no love for the child she has borne?
But even if that were possible, I would not forget you!
See, I have written your name on the palms of my hands.

ISAIAH 49:15-16

introduction

My Mother—My Heart

WHEN YOU HEAR THE WORD *MOTHER*, what happens? Do you get a rush of love or a flare of anger? A pleasant memory or a painful flashback? No matter how you respond, this book is for you.

Maybe you feel guilty for even picking up this book. After all, in a lot of ways your mother is great. But for some reason, when you hang up the phone after talking to her, you are tense and irritable, trying for the next hour to figure out what hit you. This book is for you, too!

The mother-daughter relationship is *momplicated*—one of the most complicated, yet sacred, bonds between two people. It is complex, rich, beautiful, and sometimes painful.

As coauthors—a lay person (Debbie) and a therapist (Joan)—we have been unraveling its effects on our own lives for years. We connected through mutual friends who knew we both had a passion for God and a heart for helping women. After becoming friends and sharing our experiences, we agreed that most women continue to be affected by their relationships with their mothers. When I (Debbie) lead retreats and conferences for women, I have been surprised that the audience connects so deeply with my mother story. Many come up and tell me, "Your story is my story." As a therapist, I (Joan) find that whether I am working with Christians, Muslims, or atheists, their current problems often have roots that go back to that first relationship.

Though a woman's adult relationship with her mother may be good, there is still a little girl inside all of us who has been imprinted with things that may drive us in less-than-desirable ways today. In these pages, we will be coming from a faith-based perspective, pointing you to the truths that will leave "Godprints" in the places that have held hurt or false beliefs. We will do this through our stories and other women's stories, looking for God's grace in all of them.

You won't find any mother-bashing in this book. We are mothers ourselves. We love our children, and although we have been imperfect in our mothering, we continue to make positive strides to be better. And you won't see a formula on how to be a perfect mother because there is no such thing. What we hope you'll discover is how much of you is shaped by your mother—good and bad—and how that valuable information can bring you healing and shed light on your relationship with your mother to make it less momplicated.

Both of our mothers have been gone for years, but they are still part of us. And though they are not physically present, they are still part of our everyday lives. They are the blueprint from which our lives are built. They are woven

into the fabric of our hearts. We still find ourselves wanting
to tell them when we have exciting news, wondering what
they would think about our choices, and wishing we could
call them—one more time.

This poem by an unknown author says it perfectly:

YOUR MOTHER

Your mother is always with you . . .
she's the whisper of the leaves as you walk down the street;
she is the smell of bleach in your fresh laundered socks;
she's the cool hand on your brow when you're not well.
Your mother lives inside your laughter and
she's crystallized in every tear drop.
She's the place you come from, your first home
and she's the map you follow with every step you take.
She's your first love and your first heartbreak.
And nothing on earth can separate you.
Not time, not space, not death.

Yes, our mothers are always with us. In a perfect world,
our mothers would impart only good and beautiful messages to us. It would be ideal if our mothers always embodied
the love of God toward us, but in a fallen world with real
people, it just won't happen. Many of the beliefs, reactions,
and habits formed within us have come from our responses
to this primary and vitally important relationship. Our hope
is to lead you to a place of understanding how a mother's
imprint affects your life. No matter where you might be on

this journey of discovery regarding yourself and your mother, we hope you will find valuable information in these pages. We will address how painful aspects of the mother-daughter relationship may have impacted your sense of being precious, beautiful, safe, nurtured, and strong.

Integrating biblical truth with the latest in therapeutic practice, this book will lead you along a healing path to the safe place of knowing you are truly precious and loved. No matter how your past has affected you, God offers healing, a sense of value, belonging, and strength. Overcoming the painful legacy of your mother wounds is possible through God's restoring love. This book will encourage you to have compassion on yourself, offer forgiveness and compassion to your mother, and find hope in the restoring power of God.

If you are a mom, always remember that you are partnering with God in the shaping and raising of lives that were created for his purposes. You are leaving heartprints daily on your children's souls. Be careful, be prayerful, and be grateful for the calling of motherhood, quite possibly the highest calling of all. Receive your own healing from God, accept his love for you, and let God's heart beat through yours—to those precious ones who call you Mom. Who you are stays with them forever and is passed on to the next generation. It is never too late to love, never too late to heal, and never too late to trust God to turn the pain in your story into a redemption song.

We are praying for you and asking God to be present as you read this book!

Debbie Alsdorf and Joan Edwards Kay

Debbie, nearly three and a half, and her mother.

Annie (left), six, with Aunt Betty, and Joan (right), nine, with her mother. Johnny is in the far background.

how to use this book

THIS BOOK IS MEANT TO be a healing journey. It can be done individually, in a group setting, or one-on-one with a mentor, counselor, or therapist. As you read this book, please keep the following things in mind:

- *You can either read this book lightly for the concepts or do a deep dive and incorporate the exercises. Healing is like peeling an onion; it happens one layer at a time. Go to the depth you feel is appropriate for you.*
- *If you are a mother, you will read with dual awareness. You will not only have insights about your relationship with your mother, but you will also probably see ways you have been less than perfect with your own children. If your children are still young, this book can help you change old patterns and be a better mother. If your children are now adults, remember it is never too late to work toward healing.*

- *If you have been adopted or raised by someone other than your biological mother, you may find yourself thinking about more than one mother figure as you read. Include these people as you reflect on your story.*
- *If your mother is no longer living, consider whether there might still be healing to do within yourself.*
- *Even if you and your mother have a good adult relationship now, the imprinting you received as a child may still need attention. Childhood wounds sometimes linger until we are strong enough to deal with them and let them truly heal.*
- *Try to be aware of what is happening in your body and emotions as you read the stories in this book. Your reactions can be helpful clues.*

Every woman has her own story. The specific events and memories of your life are unique to you. The level of trauma in your life is unique to you. Nevertheless, it can be helpful to look at general patterns as they are illustrated in the lives of others. Though the stories we present in this book are different from yours, you may find strands of your story as you read.

All stories in this book, unless otherwise noted, are composites. Names and details have been changed to protect confidentiality.

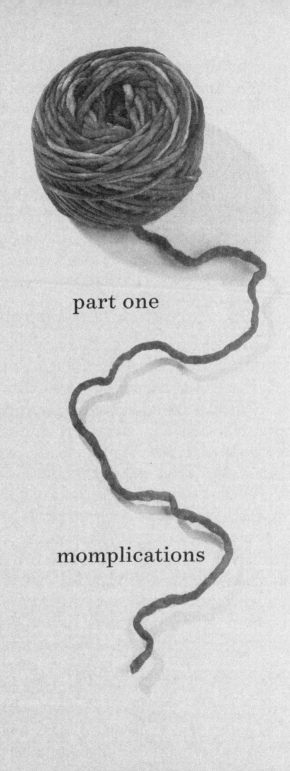

part one

momplications

The important people in our lives leave imprints. They may stay or go in the physical realm, but they are always there in your heart, because they helped form your heart. There's no getting over that.

RACHEL COHN AND DAVID LEVITHAN,
Dash and Lily's Book of Dares

1

every woman has a story

Owning our story and loving ourselves through that process is the bravest thing that we will ever do.

BRENÉ BROWN

"DEBRA, STOP WHINING OR I'll give you something to whine about. You aren't sick; you're just hungry."

"No, Mama, I'm not hungry. My tummy feels like it's stabbing me."

The arguments over my stomach pain went on for months. Even though I made frequent trips to the school nurse, my mom wasn't convinced that something could actually be physically wrong with me. She brushed it off as my need for attention.

Finally, she relented and took me to the doctor. Tests confirmed that I wasn't suffering from mere hunger pangs or trying to get my mom to notice me. It wasn't something I imagined in my head. In fourth grade, I was diagnosed with ulcers.

For my mother, this wasn't acceptable.

"You are sick all the time just like your daddy! If you weren't so nervous, your tummy would be fine. Why are you so afraid? What's wrong with you? You are dramatic and making yourself sick!"

What does a ten-year-old say to that?

I didn't know why I was sick. I didn't want to be cooped up in the office with the school nurse instead of playing outside at recess with my friends. Mom accused me of being weak because I had stomach issues. She didn't do weak, and she prided herself on being healthy and strong. She ruled our roost. As the saying goes, if Mama ain't happy, ain't nobody happy.

When I think of growing up with my mother, there are three words that come to mind—*distant*, *cold*, and *angry*. And a fourth: *longing*. I longed for her love. Although she was well liked by her coworkers and friends, her daily criticisms of me—from the way I looked to how I acted—became the way I learned to view myself. She worked the night shift and slept during school hours, but in the short daily moments we were together, she seemed irritated, distant, and uninterested. I grew up thinking I was a nuisance.

As soon as my mother heard the doctor's diagnosis, she seemed to start picking me apart about everything. It began with the ulcers, then landed on a recent portrait of me that a family friend had taken.

"What's wrong with you in this picture?"

I hesitated, frozen by her disapproving tone.

Finally I said, "I guess I'm ugly?"

My dad usually didn't get involved when my mom was mean to me, but this time he jumped in. "You are always criticizing her. Can you lay off? Just give the kid a break! She looks fine in that picture."

As much as I appreciated my dad's attempt to be my advocate, it was like adding gasoline to a fire. Mom's ranting escalated until I couldn't take it any longer. I ran out of the room, holding my hands over my ears to muffle her yells.

"Go ahead and get out of here. Your father always makes excuses for you. Why don't you just go play on the freeway!"

It wasn't the first time I had heard that last flippant remark. We lived in a tiny two-bedroom house in a beach town close to Los Angeles. There were freeways nearby, so in my little-girl mind I translated my mom's directive as "Just get lost or get hit by a car."

I had no idea what I had done to enrage my mom. I just knew I must be bad, wrong, weak, ugly, and a bother. As my parents continued to argue, I tried to make myself as small as possible on my bed in my room, hugging my knees to my chest.

When things quieted down, I snuck out without them noticing, crossed the busy four-lane street we lived on, and sat on the bench at the bus stop located across from our house. The sound of the passing cars gave me relief. I watched as people drove by and found myself thinking, *What would it be like to have a mom who liked me and didn't yell at me so much? A mom who held me when I was sick and told me I was pretty?*

I didn't have money to take the bus anywhere, but I wished that someone could take me away to a place where I would feel wanted. My stomach was churning and the tears fell freely as I kept thinking, *What is so wrong with me that even my mom and dad fight about me?*

I wish this weren't my story. These kinds of life-shaping wounds go deep. My mother left her imprint on me, and it shaped me. And though it wasn't all bad, I have spent years understanding the impact and unraveling the pain. But despite the pain, the mother-daughter relationship is deep in loyalty, even in the midst of confusing signals. My mom, the only mother I will ever have, the woman whose aloofness and criticisms hurt me, was still the woman I loved and longed for. She wasn't perfect, but she was mine.

EVERY STORY IS UNIQUE

Every daughter's story with her mother is unique. As I (Joan) read Debbie's story, I find myself comparing—noticing all the ways my mother was different from hers. I don't remember my mom criticizing or yelling at me. I wasn't afraid of her. She never told me to go play on the freeway.

No, my story with my mother is not the same as Debbie's. When I think of my mother, my stomach clenches and my throat closes. I'm aware of sadness, anger, longing, regret—a whole jumble of emotions. And there is guilt. How can I have these feelings about my mom? She did so much for me. How can I be so ungrateful?

I quickly search for positive memories to prove that I do love and appreciate my mother, and they are easy to find. My mother was a 1950s housewife. She loved to cook and prepared a delicious, balanced dinner every night. Every week she did my laundry and placed neatly folded clothes on the stairs that led to my room. We lived modestly in our 1,500-square-foot suburban home in the Midwest, but it felt abundant. I freely roamed the neighborhood to visit friends and rode my bicycle to the park. If I fell and scraped my knee or was frightened by a dog, I could run home and my mother would comfort me.

When my mother wasn't busy with a project—creating a new watercolor, planting flowers along our garage, or refinishing an old chest of drawers—she would gravitate to her favorite chair, where she sat reading for hours. During the summer, my mother took my sister, my brother, and me to the library every week so we could each get a fresh stack of books to read.

The neighborhood kids often gathered at our house because my mother allowed us to spread out and make a mess. We could turn the large room at the back of our house into a school for our dolls. We could pile the patio furniture on the lawn to build a fort. Lake Michigan was a mile away, and my mother regularly took us to the beach. In the early days, my mother seemed happy, and I felt the same way—until the year I turned nine.

It was March 22, 1961. It seemed like any other school day as I came downstairs to make myself a bowl of cereal. My grandmother was standing at the kitchen sink. She had been with us a lot recently so our mother could visit our dad in the hospital. He was there, our mother had told us, because he had an "ulcer."

My grandmother inhaled sharply when she saw me. Her usually kind face looked strained and exhausted. "Your mommy wants to see you."

I walked down the short hall to my parents' bedroom. On the bed, my mother looked disheveled in a crumpled, sleeveless nightgown, her short brown hair sticking up from the back of her head. My six-year-old sister, Annie, and four-year-old brother, Johnny, were on the bed with her, but I focused on my mother's red eyes.

"Joanie," she said, "come here. There's something I have to tell you." I warily approached and sat down.

"Last night Daddy died."

She blurted out the words, hid her face in a wad of Kleenex, and sobbed.

I went numb. *Daddy died.* I mentally repeated the words, trying to make sense of them. My dad—his warm hugs, his prickly whiskers, his twinkling eyes and half smile when he teased me—what did that mean, he had died?

I looked at my mother, hoping for understanding or comfort, but she offered nothing. She looked at me with wide, pleading eyes as if I could somehow help her. I had never seen her like this, and it was terrifying. Johnny was crying now too, and Annie's face was frozen, expressionless. I felt completely alone.

During the days that followed, I wandered, dazed, through the rubble that remained of my life. Everything was different. Our grandmother became our mom, cooking and doing laundry and making sure we got on the school bus. People continually came to our front door, where my grandmother or aunt would graciously thank them for the card or the food they had brought and tell them my mother was "sleeping." My friends were kind, but they wanted to play, not realizing that I couldn't turn away from the never-ending, screaming pain inside me. On the school playground, groups of kids huddled, whispering and looking at me. I felt achingly alone. It seemed that no one could enter my world—no one could understand. My sister and brother were too little, my aunt and grandmother were busy, my father was gone, and my mother was a stranger sitting in a green armchair, staring out the window, smoking cigarettes.

Every family and every culture has unspoken rules. My relatives approached hardship with a "stiff upper lip." The rules were "Don't talk about your pain. Don't talk about your feelings. Don't touch. Be strong and go on with life." No one held me or sat and talked with me. No one invited me to pour out my pain. It was as if I were supposed to pretend I didn't remember or care that my dad ever existed.

As spring became summer and then fall, life took on a new normal routine. My aunt went back to New York, and my grandmother returned to her house in a nearby town. However, part of our new normal was a growing awareness that Johnny was sick. I have flashes of memories—his chubby cheeks from the cortisone treatment, his wheelchair, the nosebleed that wouldn't stop—but no one said the words *cancer* or *leukemia*. I was oblivious. Annie and I were immersed in school, piano lessons, ballet classes, and friends.

By December, my mother was at the hospital with Johnny most of the time, and my grandmother came to stay with Annie and me. She made sure my sister had a birthday party when she turned seven, but Annie grieved that our mother wasn't there.

On January 29, ten months after my father's death, I got off the school bus and immediately knew something terrible had happened. There were cars in the driveway, and through the front windows I could see people in the living room. My mother met me at the door.

"Joanie, Johnny died today." The way she blurted it out reminded me of when she had told me about my father. A cold, icy rage gripped me. Anger at her, anger at the situation, anger at all those people in the living room.

As an adult, I am horrified by all my mother had to bear—losing a husband while having a terminally ill son— and I have compassion for her. But as a ten-year-old, I didn't understand. Why couldn't she make things better? I held her responsible for allowing this chaos and pain to enter my life.

I felt abandoned by her. I hadn't understood why she focused so much time and attention on Johnny in the months after our father died, but not on me and my sister. Johnny was sick, but weren't we hurting too? It makes sense to me now; what mother wouldn't spend every possible moment at the hospital with her dying son? But at the time I believed she didn't care about me, and it hurt. And over the top of that hurt, there was anger.

I punished her by pushing her away, even when she tried to be more present to me after Johnny died. The more I rejected her, the more ingratiating she became to try to win back my love, like a puppy begging to be petted. When she groveled, I rebuffed her more. I became the "alpha" in the relationship, and I hated it. I wanted her to be stronger than I was and to stop me from hurting her.

Writing about my mother is hard, yet I know there is value in honestly looking at how she continues to influence me today. She left me with countless gifts. My early years gave me a strong foundation. I was given core beliefs that I am lovable, valuable, and capable. Through her I learned the love of art and books and gardening. But she also left me with wounds.

Her emotional abandonment imprinted me with a way of approaching life and relationships that says, "You are on your own. You have only yourself to rely on. Let people get close, but not too close. Don't ever give anyone the power to hurt you by abandoning you." These messages are getting fainter and God's voice is getting louder as I walk the path of healing, but the imprint is deep in my being.

YESTERDAY'S IMPRINTS IMPACT TODAY

All of us have a story, a path, and a process that have led us to this point. Some women are very aware that their early relationships shaped them, while others are in denial about the way the messages of their past impact them today. You may not have experienced anything as traumatic with your mother as we did with ours. But if you are honest with yourself, we think you might admit there may be momplicated issues. And though we are not to live blaming our "stuff" on our mothers or on our pasts, it does serve us well to be open enough to look to the past, identifying patterns of behavior and attitude that may have been formed there.

The goal is to be able to move beyond our pasts into the future that God has designed for us. He is writing our stories. His signature is on your life and ours. Ask him to give you wisdom about why you get reactive or get stuck in ruts that are hard to get out of.

For the two of us, the path to healing has been fragmented and has come in seasons. There was never one explosive aha moment to healing and change. This healing journey with the Lord is a beautiful path to freedom that happens as he unravels it layer by layer. We are sure we will still be growing until the day that we take our last breath on earth.

As we look at our lives now, we realize that God has been shaping us since day one. He was with us in our less-than-ideal moments and in our pain. Once we could grasp that truth, it became much easier to give the pain to Jesus for healing.

He knows our hot buttons and the things that trigger our insecurity, shame, and fear. While we came from different families, we both learned dysfunctional patterns when we were young. These unhealthy patterns led to people-pleasing, compulsive overachieving, and running to food and other distractions to numb our pain. When we could look honestly at those behaviors and realize that Jesus understands every bit of dysfunction and desires to make us whole, we were able to begin our journeys to freedom from negative imprints. There has been much healing since, and there will be much more to come.

YOUR STORY

We've told you part of our stories; what about you? Take a moment to think about your mother. What comes to mind as you think about your relationship with her? What memories surface? What desires, concerns, or regrets? How do you think your relationship with your mother shaped you? It never ceases to amaze us how helpful it can be for women to address their mother relationships.

Staci wanted to meet to talk about life, spiritual growth, and mentoring, but the conversation turned to the subject of her mom. Though they had a loving relationship, Staci admitted it was strained. She had no idea how deep her daughter pain actually went until she was asked to do a presentation for her mother's sixtieth birthday. She tried to write something that would be honoring and tell the story of an amazing mom. After all, wasn't she amazing? Everyone else seemed to think so.

But Staci couldn't pen sincere words no matter how hard she tried. As she sat with her open journal in our counseling session, tears rolled down her cheeks. She went home, and when she began writing, she filled the blank pages with words that revealed all the hurt in their relationship.

The truth was that her mother had been a constant source of pain, confusion, and hurt—for years. Her mother was cold and unaffectionate. The critical spirit in which she approached everything about Staci had deeply wounded Staci's self-confidence. Naturally these cathartic realizations were not spoken at her mother's birthday party, but they were used by God as Staci began to journal, for the first time, about the effects of their relationship.

Rather than making her angry and bitter at her mom, the more Staci wrote, the more pain was released, and the healing between the two of them began. Staci became clear on what she needed to ask God for—healing from the effects of her mother's criticisms.

When we approach God with the details of our lives and stories, he meets us right there at the crossroads of the story line. He desires truth in our inward parts, and being able to face the truth brings a healing we might not have realized we needed. Staci is a very functional and successful adult. She is talented, and most people would think she was confident. But under her exterior confidence was a wound that had her secretly dwelling in insecurity and fear. She had lived her entire adult life doubting herself and letting others walk all over her.

When Staci realized how deeply her mother's criticisms had affected her, it was a game changer. She honored her mother at the party but kept it short and sweet, focusing on the many things her mother had done to help other people. After Staci sat down and exchanged smiles with her mother, she knew God was doing something powerful within her. It all began with remembering her mother-daughter story. Now that Staci was an adult, it was no longer about blaming her mother. It was now about bringing the past pain to God, who had the power to heal her in the deepest part of her soul. This allowed her to honor her mother at the celebration while receiving peace directly from God in the process.

Explore Your Story

1. Take some time and write out a rough first draft of your mother story. What incidents and memories first appear in your mind? What are the defining moments? Don't filter or edit or try to put them in any order at this point; just write them as they come—the good and the bad. Don't worry about anyone seeing it; this is just for you and your own personal discovery and healing. Keep in mind that this may be difficult, and it may hurt more than you

expect, so be kind to yourself. Before you dive in, you may want to prepare in a way that will honor this process—go somewhere beautiful or make yourself a cup of tea.

2. What physically happens in your body and what emotions immediately surface when you think of your mother? What is your "gut level" reaction?

3. Come up with three words that describe your mother's positive qualities (for example, *nurturing, smart, creative*) and three words that describe her negative qualities (for example, *cold, controlling, preoccupied*).

4. How did your mother comfort you (or not) when you were hurting—physically or emotionally?

Connect with God

Lord, as I begin this journey, I ask you to be with me as I process my memories and pain from the past. Take the blinders off my eyes and help me to see clearly. I do not want to linger in any toxic emotions, but if they surface, please help me remember to bring those ugly feelings to you. Grant me courage, grace, and strength as I look to you for healing. Help me seek your truth as I examine the messages received by my little-girl heart that have followed me into my big-girl life and relationships. I trust you. Amen.

2

every woman has an imperfect mother

There are no perfect moms,
just imperfect ones partnering with a perfect God.

JILL SAVAGE

THERE IS NO PERFECT MOTHER. Most mothers love their children and do the best they can with the tools they have been given. However, as mothers, we are all human, and as much as we would like to stay in our loving, wise, adult selves as we parent our children, we all have times when something triggers us and we become reactive.

Daniel Siegel and Mary Hartzell, in their book *Parenting from the Inside Out*, have suggested that parents relate to their children from either the "high road" or the "low road" and typically move back and forth between the two.[1] On the high road, parents are mindful and attuned to their children, responding in ways that are loving and healthy. On the low road, they "lose it," get carried away by their own unresolved issues, and react emotionally in ways that are not in their children's best interest.

Angela was your typical "trying to do her best" mom, spinning many plates in the air while trying to be present for her children. Her own mother had lacked in the "togetherness and being there for her kids" department, so Angela vowed never to do that to her own children. But when Angela was diagnosed with a life-threatening illness, she was down for the count. The medications made her tired, her emotions were dark and moody, and as a mother she began to check out. Adults understood she was going through a rough spot, but her children couldn't figure out why Mommy was always snapping at them and didn't want to spend time with them.

One day while wrestling with discouragement, Angela realized that since being diagnosed, she had isolated herself from little hearts that needed to grasp what Mommy was going through. Angela became acutely aware of how much her behavior mimicked her own mother's interactions with Angela and her siblings, albeit for different reasons.

Angela had a choice to make. Either she could continue to check out or she could help her children understand why Mommy was acting differently. She ultimately chose the high road and invited the children into her bed, where she read to them, allowed them to rub her feet or head when she was feeling terrible, and assured them how special they were to her. Angela's children became part of the journey with her—making cards, helping Dad with meals, and giving Mom lots of extra snuggles and hugs. The door that was initially shut to the kids was now open, and they all ended up stronger because of it.

If you are a mother, please forgive yourself for the times you have been on the low road. All mothers go there at times, and all mothers wound their children—sometimes in big ways, sometimes in minor ways. Rather than sitting in self-condemnation or regret, make it your goal to heal your own wounds and spend more time on the high road. It is never too late. The very best thing you can do to help your children heal is to heal yourself. From the high road, you can repair any damage you may have done, even if your children are now adults.

THE TRUTH IS . . . IT'S MOMPLICATED

Our relationships with our mothers are rich, complex, and momplicated. And yet it can be difficult to fully understand why they are that way. Why can't we readily recognize the effects and identify what needs to be fixed? What might be preventing us from seeing clearly? Here are eight reasons why the effects of this important relationship might be obscured.

1. **Things are good between our mothers and us at the moment.**

One of the top reasons you may not see your past clearly is if your current relationship with your mother is good. Remember that your relationship with your mother has been lifelong. It is likely that your mother has changed since you were a child. The following story of Amber illustrates how a good adult-to-adult relationship does not necessarily mean that wounds from childhood are healed.

Amber is thirty years old and has a child of her own. She had been in therapy for more than a year to heal her relationship with her mother, strategizing how to confront her, learning to set healthy boundaries, and finding ways to reconnect with her. Her mother had also been in therapy and made significant changes. Now that her mother has become part of her life again and is an involved grandmother, Amber believes her mother issues are resolved.

However, when Amber and her husband recently got into a heated argument and he said he needed to take a walk to calm down, she exploded in rage. As he opened the door to leave, Amber followed him and tried to block his way, screaming at him to not leave. She lost all self-control, angrily calling him names while desperately wanting him to come back and soothe her.

Amber was chronologically an adult, but she reacted like a five-year-old. She experienced the panic and loneliness she had felt as a child when her mother would leave her and her younger brother at home alone. Her husband's action reminded Amber of that abandonment, causing her wounded daughter self to surface. While her adult self gets along well with her mother, a younger part of her still holds feelings of anxiety and terror.

2. **We are grateful for all the ways our mothers have gifted us.**

The damage or hurt caused by our mothers is often obscured because of the many ways they have blessed and gifted us. Your mother may have hurt you, yet she gave you life. At times she may be your biggest critic; at others she may be your biggest fan. At times she may be cold and angry; at others she may be warm and nurturing. Mothers are complex human beings with histories, trauma, fears, and hopes. And mothers relate to their daughters out of all that complexity.

Chelsea's parents divorced when she was young. Her mother remained loving and attentive to her daughter's needs, but because of her own hurt, Chelsea's mother was not discreet in the things she shared about Chelsea's father. She cast her ex-husband in a negative light and discouraged her daughter from having a healthy relationship with him. Dad was a good guy, but the divorce was ugly, and Mom transferred all that ugliness into her daughter's mind.

The contempt and lies Chelsea's mother expressed seemed normal to Chelsea in childhood. But it caused distance between her and her dad and increased her anxiety about not being loved enough by him.

This anxiety affects her adult relationships, especially with men. She has unrealistic expectations and is easily hurt and disappointed when those expectations are not met. Chelsea doesn't see this as an issue that connects with her mother because her mother has always been so loving and attentive toward her. But even though Chelsea's mother was kind to her, she hurt Chelsea by the way she spoke to her about her father.

3. **We never stop longing for our mothers' love.**

Young children depend on their mothers for their very survival. They need their mothers to meet their core needs, to feed them, and to keep them safe. The thought of being without Mother is intolerable. A child cannot bear to question the goodness or stability of someone she needs so profoundly. Rather than facing the terrifying and chaotic possibility that her mother might be flawed, a daughter blames herself and assumes she is flawed or has done something wrong.

The God-given impulse to go to our mothers for love and comfort compels adult women to keep at it. They continue to revisit that maternal well even when it is dry, hoping that this time things will be different.

Peg Streep described this dilemma of adult women who are trying to face the reality of their mother wounds:

> Grieving the mother you needed is impeded by . . . what I call the *core conflict*. This conflict is between the daughter's growing awareness of how her mother wounded her in childhood, and still does, *and* her continuing need for maternal love and support, even in adulthood. This pits the [daughter's] need to save and protect herself against the continuing hope that, somehow, she can figure out what she can do to get her mother to love her.[2]

4. **We have compassion for the difficulties our mothers endured.**

When we realize our mothers faced difficulties, we may think it insensitive to acknowledge our wounds. I (Joan) struggled with this. How could I blame my mother for anything after she lost her husband and son? It is always helpful to learn your mother's story— her upbringing, her hurts, her struggles. When you see her more clearly, you can free yourself from self-blame. *It wasn't because I was bad that she ignored me. It was because she was depressed.* Understanding Mom's story can also be a step toward compassion and forgiveness. However, the fact that your mother faced personal trials does not remove the reality that your needs were not met. The goal is to be able to hold compassion for Mom, while still telling the truth about times you were hurt or affected negatively. We must honestly face reality and hold both truths at the same time—our mothers need compassion, and our hurts need acknowledgment so they can be healed.

5. **Some wounds do not seem like wounds.**

Some patterns that result from our relationships with our mothers impair us, but they don't seem like wounds. A wound is defined as "damage, hurt, or injury." If a daughter has been brought up with the belief that she is better than everyone else or entitled to special treatment, she may not feel hurt or injured, but she has still been damaged. A mind-set of pride, superiority, or entitlement will get in the way of good relationships with other people and God. It will, at some point, bring her pain. It can be hard to see that this, too, is a kind of wound.

Linda's mother was a high-profile leader in her church, respected by all. She expected Linda to live up to her high standards and to represent their family well. Linda rose to the challenge and did almost everything perfectly. She got good grades, was elected to student council, and had an impressive résumé of community service. She never suspected she carried mother wounds.

However, Linda's mother would often speak of

other families with disdain, pointing out how they were not doing things as well as her own family did. Linda developed a subtle attitude of prideful superiority that made other people pull away from her. She wondered why she didn't have more friends. Almost everyone respected her, but not everyone enjoyed her company. When she was challenged to examine how her mother's pride had affected her, she saw the generational tendency, repented, and began to humbly and openly admit her own areas of brokenness. As she became softer and more authentic, her relationships became more intimate and fulfilling. Some wounds don't feel like wounds, but they are.

6. **Some wounds come from too much "love" or too much involvement.**

It is counterintuitive to think of wounding that is caused by too much attention from one's mother, yet overinvolvement and doing too much for a daughter can harm her just as neglect can.

Everyone described Hazel's mother as "sweet" and agreed that "she wouldn't hurt a fly." She made sure Hazel's every need was met. She doted on her, cooking for her, cleaning her room, doing her laundry, and treating her like a princess. While that kind of care was good for Hazel when she was young, it impaired her as she got older. She expected others to put their needs aside and attend to hers, just as her mother always did. She waited for others to take care of things, rather than being responsible herself. Hazel would not have described herself as wounded by her mother; she insisted that she was loved. But the truth is that her mother's "love" caused her to become lazy. This handicapped her growth and prevented her from becoming independent as she grew up. Some of the patterns she developed in relationship with her mother now get in the way of her being the loving, capable person God designed her to be.

7. **We can't remember our early years.**

Most of us have spotty memories of our childhoods. Childhood amnesia—the loss of most early memories by the time we are seven—is a real phenomenon. Scientists are not sure why it occurs, but they theorize it has to do with how the brain is growing and changing. Even after age seven, memories tend to fade unless they are connected to deep emotions or have been revisited through photographs or family storytelling.

Try to be aware of what is happening in your body and emotions as you read the stories in this book. Your reactions may be clues to your past. Also, consider doing some research, interviewing those who were present when you were young, looking through family photo albums, and praying that God would reveal what needs to be revealed.

As I (Joan) started this project with Debbie, I held the belief that my mother had been disconnected and had left me alone to fend for myself. It was a story I told myself based on the memories that were most vivid in my mind. However, as I went through old photos, I found one of my mother smiling and standing behind me with her arms around me. A strong memory came back to me, so strong I could remember her warmth against my back and the happiness I had felt. Looking at that picture, I couldn't hold on to my old, negative story anymore. Yes, there were times I felt abandoned, but there were also many times I felt loved and connected. I felt deep remorse for my disrespect and negativity toward my mother. The photos helped me remember, and the memories helped me melt an unforgiving, frozen place in my heart.

8. **We have a natural denial system.**

We don't want to think about painful things. Denial is the protective mechanism that allows us to tolerate the intolerable. When experiences or feelings are so difficult that we feel as if we won't survive them, we seal them up and shut them off from our consciousness. In cases of extreme abuse, it is a blessing for children to be able to bury their memories. Sometimes God brings the recollections back when the child is old enough to handle them. Sometimes they never emerge, which may be best overall. It's similar to a doctor deciding to leave a bullet in someone's body rather than attempting risky surgery. However, God wants truth to illuminate our inward parts. In most cases, it is worth the pain of facing the things we have hidden from ourselves so we can bring them to God for healing and be free of their effects.

When I (Debbie) started counseling, we began to delve into the subject of my mother's lack of affection for me, and I started to experience new understanding and inner healing. During this time, my whole family came down with the stomach flu. For my entire adult life, it had been well known to my family that I did not throw up. In fact, I hadn't thrown up in fifty years. But to my surprise, this time I got sick like everyone else—retching sick.

As I lay in bed in disbelief that I had actually thrown up, a long-forgotten memory popped onto the screen of my mind. I was about eleven years old and had the stomach flu. My mom didn't want to clean up a mess, so she told me to go out on the front porch and lie there until I was done throwing up. Since we lived on a busy street, I was humiliated, fearing someone would see me. The whole experience was so traumatic for me that deeply buried pain and shame had blocked me from being able to get sick all these years. Now, decades later, God was bringing healing. It seems funny to think of throwing up as healing, but doing so is a normal bodily process that provides relief. I have since gotten sick one other time and was reminded that God indeed had healed this part of me. The pain of my past was no longer blocking me.

Traumatic experiences can be stored in our subconscious minds, but God is powerful and can bring them to light and heal them in his time.

If you have a history of serious abuse or neglect, pray that God would guide your healing. Pray that he would reveal only the memories you are ready for. Trust him on this. He is the best counselor, and his timing is perfect.

As you read through these eight reasons your momplications might be obscured, did any of them resonate with you? It can be difficult to see how we have been hurt. But when we are willing to acknowledge what's happened and how it has affected us, God promises to help us achieve emotional healing.

ASSESSMENT: IDENTIFYING THE MOMPLICATIONS

To explore the effect of mother-daughter dynamics even more, we have put together a self-assessment. The following questions are designed to help you continue to identify areas where you possibly received less-than-perfect mothering. Be aware that it could be challenging. Some descriptions could bring back painful memories you've forgotten. Others may serve as reminders that healing has taken place or is already in process. But in our experience and research, we've found that if you don't acknowledge the wounds, they are likely to pop up at unexpected times, possibly when you are in an intimate relationship or when you become a parent.

This is for your eyes only, and we encourage you to answer honestly. Use the assessment as a tool rather than a scientific evaluation. As you explore each area, we pray God brings you awareness of where your mother fell short—not for the purpose of mother-bashing, but in order for you to heal. Identifying a problem is the first step toward growth and change. This will take time and effort but will be well worth it.

Our hope is that you will begin to free yourself from destructive patterns and pain that have been barriers for you. Once these barriers have been broken, God's joy and peace can fill your heart. As Ann Voskamp wrote, "Wounds are what break open the soul to plant the seeds of a deeper growth."[3]

We have arranged the questions into groups of related issues and listed the chapters that specifically address those topics. Of course, we want you to read the entire book, but feel free to experience it at your own pace and in light of your personal experiences.

You may find yourself answering yes to many of the questions. It can be overwhelming to be confronted with all the momplicated places at once, but we ask you to keep going. You will be rating your responses differently for each question. Take the first question: "Were there times when you longed for your mother's physical presence, but she was not there for you?" We can all say there has been a time we have longed for our mother's physical presence. For that reason, we encourage you to give a number between 0 and 10 that represents the intensity of your response to each question. If your mother died when you were five years old, the answer to this first question may feel like a 10. If she forgot to pick you up after school one time, you may still answer yes, but it may only feel like a 1 on the momplicated scale. If you feel as if God has already healed that area of your heart, the rating may be lower than if it's still a pressing issue. The intensity of your experiences and the frequency with which things happened are factors in how you will pick your number.

Don't overthink this evaluation. Read the question, let the memories come, and write down the number you feel at a gut level.

The overarching question to ask yourself before you score is this:

On a scale from 0 to 10, how painful/concerning/disturbing is this question to me?

Remember, nothing can be healed that is not first acknowledged. This is your first step on a journey that will lead you to greater joy and freedom.

momplication #1:

Was Your Mother Present?

_____ 1. Were there times when you longed for your mother's physical presence, but she was not there for you?

_____ 2. Has your mother ever left you alone when you were hurting, sad, or afraid?

_____ 3. Were there times you went to your mother for comfort, but she did not provide it?

_____ 4. Have you wished your mother were warmer or more nurturing, or that she touched or hugged you more?

_____ 5. Have you wished your mother were more able to hear you, understand you, see you?

_____ 6. Have you experienced longing when you have seen how other mothers treat their daughters?

We discuss why a present and attuned mother is crucial for a daughter in chapter 5. Suggestions for healing can be found in chapters 5, 9, and 10.

momplication #2:

Did Your Mother Keep You Safe?

_____ 1. Were there times when you did not feel physically or emotionally safe with your mother?

_____ 2. Was your mother unpredictable or did she have a pattern of losing control of her emotions?

_____ 3. Has your mother lied to you or made promises she didn't keep?

_____ 4. Did your mother allow you to be exposed to sexual things that were inappropriate for your age?

_____ 5. Were there times when you felt your mother should have protected you from others, but she did not?

We address the importance of a safe, protective, emotionally regulated mother in chapter 6. Suggestions for healing can be found in chapters 6, 9, and 10.

momplication #3:

Did Your Mother Teach and Guide You?

_____ 1. Rather than setting healthy limits on you, did your mother let you have inappropriate control?

_____ 2. When you were young, did you ever feel as if you were your mother's parent, needing to comfort or counsel her?

_____ 3. Has your mother modeled or allowed unethical behavior?

_____ 4. Has your mother tried to dress like you or be a part of your group of friends or flirted with your boyfriends?

_____ 5. Were there areas in which your mother neglected to give you important instruction or guidance?

_____ 6. Has your mother seemed like a defeated victim of life rather than a victor?

We look at the importance of having a mother who takes the parental role, providing instruction and leadership and establishing limits, in chapter 7. Suggestions for healing can be found in chapters 7, 9, and 10.

momplication #4:

Did Your Mother Celebrate You as a Unique Individual?

_____ 1. Has your mother been critical?

_____ 2. Has your mother been controlling, overbearing, or overprotective?

_____ 3. Has your mother discouraged you from pursuing your own interests, wanting to choose your life path for you?

_____ 4. Has your mother discouraged you from expressing your emotions or opinions, expecting them to be like hers?

_____ 5. Has it seemed that you existed to serve your mother or care for her?

We discuss why it's important for a mother to celebrate the ways in which her daughter is valuable and different from her in chapter 8. Suggestions for healing can be found in chapters 8, 9, and 10.

Momplication #5:

Did Your Mother Negatively Shape Your Self-Image?

_____ 1. Has your mother called you "stupid, "lazy," "fat," or other demeaning names?

_____ 2. Has your mother conveyed to you that you are not lovable or that you don't have value?

_____ 3. Have your interactions with your mother left you believing you are "not enough"?

_____ 4. Has your mother openly criticized women's appearances or bodies (including her own, yours, or other women's)?

_____ 5. Has your mother given you unhealthy messages about how to relate to men?

_____ 6. Has your mother blamed you for things you didn't deserve the blame for?

Throughout the book, we examine the lies we come to believe through our relationships with our mothers and the truths that refute and heal them. However, chapters 9 and 10 are particularly focused on the steps to healing imprinted negative beliefs.

Momplication #6:

Do You Struggle in Your Current Relationship with Your Mother?

If you struggle in your current relationship with your mother, chances are there are patterns that began early in your relationship. However, the struggles we have today are often what drive us toward healing.

_____ 1. Has it seemed that no matter what you do, you cannot give your mother enough time to satisfy her?

_____ 2. If you are a mother, has your mother tried to tell you how to raise your own children or competed with you for your children's love and attention?

_____ 3. Has your mother gotten jealous when you have tried to pursue close friendships with other women?

_____ 4. As your mother has gotten older, has she been ungrateful or critical toward you?

_____ 5. As an adult, do you wish your mother were more supportive or present for you?

Chapter 11 contains suggestions for how to deal with our adult relationships with our mothers.

In Psalm 139:23, David asked God to survey and reveal what he found on the landscape of David's heart. "Search me, O God, and know my heart." Consider making this a continual prayer for yourself going forward. God knows your story better than anyone and is there when the details seem too hard and complicated to face. He is the one who heals, restores, and redeems—making things beautiful in his time.

Explore Your Story

1. Ask yourself, "Have I been avoiding acknowledging how my mother's actions or words have affected me? Have I been guilty of hiding behind a reason not to explore that pain?"

2. If you haven't already taken the assessment "Identifying the Momplications," please take time to do so.

3. Pick one question that had a higher score and that stands out to you.

   Journal about the memories, thoughts, and feelings that question evokes. Don't edit yourself; just write whatever comes to mind.

Ask God to reveal to you how this wound might be impacting your adult life. What might be the ongoing effects? What has truly been healed? What has not?

Connect with God

Heavenly Father, I thank you for the beautiful gift of being filled with your Holy Spirit. I thank you that you rescued me from sin and spiritual death. My spirit has been made new, but I have remnants of pain still residing in me. You promise to restore my soul, and I look to you for that. Give me courage to admit I have some hurtful wounds and that I struggle with ugly patterns as a result. May I be brave enough to run to you, blaming no one, grateful for all the blessings I have received, trusting in the grace and beauty of your bigger story in my life. Bring beauty to life in me, by the power of Jesus' name. Amen.

3

every woman carries
her mother's mark

*Looking back allows us to see
the imprint of where we began.*

SUZANNE ELLER

"JOANIE, YOU *ARE* YOUR MOTHER'S DAUGHTER."

My childhood friend Nancy and I stood, coffee mugs in hand, watching our newly acquainted children play in the backyard of my small house. Neighborhood children had come to join the fun, and they had rearranged the patio furniture under blankets to build a fort. Toys were strewn everywhere.

Nancy took a sip of coffee and shook her head in wonder. "This is just how it was when we were kids."

For better or for worse, we tend to imitate our mothers. We may cook our eggs . . . just the way they did. We may overbuy at Christmas . . . just the way they did. We may be argumentative . . . just the way they were. We may always remember to send birthday cards . . . just the way they did.

Why did our mothers have such a profound effect on us? Why did they have so much power to bless us or to wound us? It is because, as children, we were pliable and impressionable. The people and the circumstances of our early lives have the greatest impact on who we will become and how we will relate to the world and others. For almost every child, the first and deepest imprinting takes place in connection to his or her mother.

What are imprints? Imprints are the programming, the indelible mark someone leaves on another person. They are part of our blueprint for life—a complex engraving of good and bad and everything in between. They hold our strengths and they hold our wounds. They exist in the realm of beliefs and also on physical levels that include our bodies, the structure and functioning of our brains, and our nervous systems. Our early experiences sear patterns into our souls as powerfully as a hot branding iron, and these patterns can influence us throughout our lives.

Mothers may leave the most profound imprints on their daughters, but we all leave lasting impressions wherever we go.

Ruth Harms Calkin captures this idea poetically in these lines from "Heartprints."

Whatever our hands touch—
We leave fingerprints!
On walls, on furniture

On doorknobs, dishes, books.
There's no escape.
As we touch we leave our identity.

O God, wherever I go today
Help me to leave heartprints!
Heartprints of compassion,
Of understanding and love.
Heartprints of kindness
And genuine concern.[1]

What a beautiful expression of good, positive imprints! Yes, our mothers have left their heartprints on us—blessings and wounds—because their lives have touched ours. While being grateful for the positive, we need to recognize what has been negative, so we can work to change the unhealthy ways we have learned to cope. When we do, we can more readily leave positive, life-giving marks on others.

IMPRINTING STARTS EARLY

Here's something difficult to wrap our minds around: Heartprints start forming from *the moment you are conceived* in your mother's womb. At that time, your mother contributes twenty-three chromosomes containing genes that give your body a blueprint for growth. These twenty-three chromosomes, combined with the twenty-three chromosomes from your father, define you genetically—your coloring, your body type, your vulnerability to certain diseases (like breast cancer or alcoholism), and your entire physical makeup.

For the nine months you are in the womb, your mother continues to have an immeasurable impact on you. If she listens to relaxing music, you get the neurochemicals that help you feel calm and relaxed. If she drinks coffee, you receive the effects of caffeine. If she is afraid, you experience the adrenaline. Your body begins to adapt to the chemical and hormonal environment she provides, whether it is nurturing and safe or stressful and dangerous.

At birth, your brain forms according to your relationship with your mother (or whoever is acting as primary caretaker). The brain grows or severs neural connections, changing structurally according to a child's relationship with Mom. If Mom is fairly responsive and reliable, the child's brain sculpts to expect safety in relationships. If Mom is neglectful, abusive, or inconsistent, the child's brain adapts and becomes hypersensitive to the possibility of danger. Before you have any words or context to describe it, your body develops an orientation to the world—an expectation of whether others will be loving and consistent or erratic, neglectful, and harmful. A relational template is laid.

As we began to work on this book and Joan began sharing these facts with me, I (Debbie) sat in amazement. Things seemed to click into place. Could my mother's inconsistency with me explain why I grew up with unreasonable fears? As strange as it sounds, I was afraid to take a shower, and I hadn't even seen the movie *Psycho*! I took baths because there was no noise from streaming water to prevent me from hearing everything around me. From a young age I didn't feel safe, but I never knew where the fear actually came from. Most of the time, the panic was unfounded, but it still overwhelmed me. This fear was my personal secret.

As Joan and I talked, I began to realize that I didn't need to blame myself or be ashamed of my fear. Interestingly enough, I took my first shower at age seventeen—the night I received Christ. For a moment, as the water flowed over me, all my anxiety washed away. To be honest, the fear has recurred off and on through my life. Now each time it occurs, I take fearful little Debbie straight to the throne of Jesus and ask him for more deep and lasting inner healing.

OUR MOTHERS' IMPRINTS
AFFECT OUR IDENTITIES

In my counseling practice, I (Joan) have become aware of how profoundly a mother impacts her daughter's life. Our earliest beliefs about ourselves start with our mothers. They are the first mirrors in which we see ourselves; we learn who we are by what we see reflected in their eyes. If they view us as precious, we believe we are precious. If they find us annoying or too much to handle, we assume that viewpoint. If they think we are better than every other child and entitled to special treatment, we adopt that self-concept.

In our early years, we don't have the ability to discern what is true from what is not. Our mothers' ideas about us leave an impression like a hand pressed into wet cement. We are highly sensitive to their emotions, actions, and words, and they engrave our souls with a working theory of who we are.

Beliefs also form from verbal cues; when we hear loving words, we begin to think *I am lovable.* But for the first few years of life, we don't have words. The parts of our brains that hold words and beliefs are still developing. This is why our healing needs to be deeper than words.

Because of her own mother's rejection, Debbie internalized the belief that she was not valuable. Her many successes in life were temporary salve but did not heal that deeply held conviction. Later in life, when she faced rejection from others, the lie that had been planted in her as a child came flooding back in full force, causing her immense pain and self-doubt.

Although Debbie was a Christian, quoting Bible verses to her at that time would have been as effective as putting a Band-Aid on a hemorrhaging wound. She knew all those verses but needed to ask God to do a deep work in her soul, replacing the core lie that she is not valuable with the truth that she is his beloved daughter and he is well pleased with her. I often hear clients say, "I know the right answer. I know the Bible teaches that I am loved (or valuable or safe or significant), but it doesn't *feel* true. I know it in my head, but not in my heart." Women who have studied the Bible for years and know its truths will often feel guilty that they can't wholeheartedly believe that they are who God says they are, or that they can't find a way to live from those truths.

Why do we experience this inner struggle? I like to imagine our souls as pieces of paper. Sometimes the truth of Scripture falls on us like ink on a fresh sheet—it is a revelation, and we can accept it with undivided joy. However, more often we are like a page filled with words; notes left by our earlier experiences may contradict or jumble the message of biblical truth. They are like ugly scribblings scratched on a beautiful page, detrimental to our spiritual lives and our relationships. When we hear Scripture at this point, it's no wonder that we can't accept the truth—there is no space to see it on the page.

Over time, I (Debbie) began to learn that we must rely on God to erase the false messages that we have believed. When thinking of our identities, we must realize that what defines us is what will drive us. Who do we think we are? How do we define our place in this world? If we define ourselves by what Scripture says about us, we will be confident and experience growing freedom in Christ—to do his will and live for him. But if not, we will constantly be measuring ourselves with a faulty ruler. We will be driven to prove ourselves, if only to ourselves. The effect of rejection or neglect is described beautifully by Henri Nouwen:

> Over the years, I have come to realize that the greatest trap in our life is not success, popularity, or power, but self-rejection. . . . When we have

come to believe in the voices that call us worthless
and unlovable, then success, popularity, and power
are easily perceived as attractive solutions. The
real trap, however, is self-rejection. . . . As soon as
someone accuses me or criticizes me, as soon as I
am rejected, left alone, or abandoned, I find myself
thinking: "Well, that proves once again that I am a
nobody." . . . My dark side says: "I am no good. . . .
I deserved to be pushed aside, forgotten, rejected,
and abandoned." Self-rejection is the greatest enemy
of the spiritual life because it contradicts the sacred
voice that calls us the "Beloved." Being the Beloved
constitutes the core truth of our existence.[2]

The lies and half-truths that have been imprinted on us
hold us in bondage to a negative and less-than-biblical self-
perception. An identity of being worthless does not align
with God's truth of our value as his creation, or more specifically for Christians, as his new creations. Throughout
the Bible, God gives people new names that represent their
new identities because of their relationships with him.
Abram became Abraham, Sarai became Sarah, and Cephas
became Peter.

It is important to identify the false messages and how they
have been affecting our adult lives. As you begin this journey,
ask God's Spirit to guide you into all truth of who he really
believes you are.

When He, the Spirit of Truth, comes, He will guide
you into all the truth [full and complete truth].

JOHN 16:13, AMP

OUR MOTHERS' IMPRINTS AFFECT OUR INTIMACY PATTERNS

"Please talk to me," April pleaded with her husband of five
years. Like most women, she longed for a husband who was
present, loving, and caring. Instead, she ended up married
to a man who remained detached and aloof, much like the
mother she grew up with.

How did I let this happen? she wondered. *How could I have
"married" my mother?*

The deep, body-level presumption of whether or not the
world is safe, of whether we can trust others to "be there"
for us and meet our needs, starts at birth and is known as an
attachment style. It is how we habitually relate to others—
our fallback pattern for intimacy or lack of intimacy. Studies
have shown that children between the ages of nine and eighteen months already tend to display one of four attachment
styles in relationship with their mothers.[3]

1. **Secure attachment:** These children have a basic trust
that Mother will "be there" for them. If their mothers
leave the room, they are distressed, but then are easily comforted when their mothers return. In general,
they are calm and happy. Because they feel that their

mothers are a safe base that they can return to at any time, they feel comfortable venturing out and exploring their worlds.

Children develop a secure attachment style when their mothers are for the most part available to meet their needs for food, comfort, and connection. Though there will be times when the mother is unavailable, the child has developed a basic trust that she will return.

2. **Anxious attachment:** These children display a highly emotional push-pull with their mothers. If the mother leaves the room and then returns, the child is difficult to console. The child wants to reach for her mother and reconnect, yet at the same time is angry that she left, sometimes even rejecting her advances. Because the child is anxious, rather than trusting that the mother will physically or emotionally be there for her, the child has a harder time moving away from the mother to explore her environment.

   This attachment style can result when a mother is inconsistent in her physical presence and care for the child. It also can result from an insensitivity to what the child is trying to convey or from anxiety in the mother herself. The mother might be preoccupied with other things or overly attentive because of her own anxieties or vacillate between the two. Children with anxious attachment seem to be more agitated than those who have secure attachment.

3. **Avoidant attachment:** These children show very little emotion and don't seem to care when their mothers leave the room. There is not a big difference between how they respond to their mothers and how they respond to strangers. When the mother returns to the room, the child tends to avoid or ignore her. Unlike the child with anxious attachment who seems to be agitated, as though there is always a foot on her emotional gas pedal, this child seems numbed, as though there is a foot on her emotional brake.

   This style develops when a mother is self-absorbed or rejecting. The child tries crying, tries engaging, seeks to have Mother "be there" for her, but eventually learns that her attempts don't yield results, so she gives up and shuts down. She may be fed and changed, but she learns to expect that her mother won't see her, play with her, or attune to her in the way she needs.

4. **Disorganized attachment:** A small number of children display behaviors that don't seem to make any sense. Their behavior is inconsistent and confusing—anxious in one moment, avoidant the next. It is as if there is a foot on the gas and a foot on the brake at the same time.

   This style is the result of abusive or scary early experiences with parents. The child has been put in a double bind because she feels compelled to go to the parent for comfort while feeling compelled to get away from the parent for safety.

If you are a young mother, be encouraged. The truth is, you don't have to be present 24-7 for your child to thrive. A generally warm, present, responsive mother will give a child a secure attachment style. A secure relationship with Dad and other adults will have a positive impact too.

When a mother doesn't meet a child's need for secure attachment, it is often because of reasons beyond her control. It may be circumstantial or due to illness. The mother may be depressed or preoccupied with a personal crisis. Most commonly, she may have never securely attached with her own mother and lacks the capacity to provide something she never received. Whatever the reason, children do their best to survive by adapting to the situation in which they find themselves.

Attachment styles impact our adult relationships. We go into the world with a working model of how we expect things to go. Attachment styles can change over time, and different attachment styles also develop with different people, but the template laid in relationship to your mother is deep and worth examining. For example, a woman with a secure attachment style might make deep friendships easily and find a trustworthy man to love; a woman with an anxious style might drive people away with her constant need for reassurance; and a woman with an avoidant style might feel lonely because she has difficulty allowing people to be close to her.

Keep in mind that our attachment styles can change over time. My (Joan's) story is an example of this. In my early years, I would have been categorized as having a secure attachment style, but when my father and brother died and my mother was not able to comfort me, I became anxious—longing for comfort from my mother, yet angrily rejecting her. Finally, as I stopped hoping for my mother's comfort, I pulled back and became avoidantly attached to her. I lost trust that she would "be there" for me emotionally and stuffed my painful feelings away.

Just as negative experiences, such as loss and trauma, can negatively impact our attachment styles and make us less secure, more positive experiences also have a huge impact. Security grows as we learn to trust other family members, teachers, close friends, spouses, and, of course, God. Our early relationships with our mothers are foundational, but they do not determine our fate.

And the best news is, we have God as our ultimate secure attachment. The Bible reveals these things about his character:

- *He cares for us as a shepherd cares for his sheep (see Psalm 23).*
- *He knows every hair on our heads (see Luke 12:7).*
- *He sees us and hears us when we cry out to him (see Psalm 34:17).*
- *He is faithful and trustworthy and will never leave us nor forsake us (see Hebrews 13:5).*

Unlike with our earthly parents, who might fail to be there for us, nothing can separate us from God's love (see Romans 8:38). The more we truly believe these truths about God, the more we will feel deep physical peace, resting like a baby who knows that her mother is not far away.

Read this passage slowly and let the truth wash over you:

Listen to me, [fill in your name here]. . . .
I have cared for you since you were born.
    Yes, I carried you before you were born.
I will be your God throughout your lifetime—
    until your hair is white with age.
I made you, and I will care for you.
    I will carry you along and save you.

ISAIAH 46:3-4

Though we were formed in our mothers' wombs, God has been with us since the moment of conception, weaving us together, upholding us, making us for his purposes. After we were born, he was the unseen one carrying us. And as we grow older, he is still with us, sustaining and guiding us.

What about you? As you've read this chapter, have any early memories come back to you? It's never too late for healing. Remember, this process is not to blame or accuse, but only to unveil areas where we still need to heal and be made whole.

Explore Your Story

1. Read through the following list of positive beliefs you might have about yourself. Be aware of how your body reacts and what thoughts come to mind in response to each one. Are there any that you logically, biblically know are true, but that don't *feel* true?

I am precious.

I am lovable.

I am valuable and have worth.

I am good enough.

I'm okay the way I am.

I am capable and can succeed.

I am honorable.

I deserve respect.

I have strength.

I have intelligence.

I am significant (important).

I am connected (not alone).

2. Spend some time thinking and praying about the beliefs that did not feel true for you. What may have caused those lies to be imprinted in your heart? Bring each one to God, asking him to show you where you have had wrong thinking, and praying that he would renew your mind.

3. Consider which attachment style you may have developed with your mother in your first two years. If they are available, ask older people who knew you as a baby (parents, grandparents, or older siblings) to describe what you were like. Were you generally happy, or did you cry a lot? Were you clingy, or were you detached? How did you respond when your mother left you with other caretakers?

4. Reflect on how you attach to other people now. Do you generally feel safe and connected, or are you tentative, insecure, or suspicious?

5. What traumatic events (losses, deaths, betrayals) throughout your life have had a negative effect on your attachment style?

6. What healing relationships (friends, communities, surrogate mothers, spouses) have had a positive effect on your attachment style?

7. What is your attachment style in relationship to God? Are you secure, anxious, or avoidant?

Connect with God

Lord, thank you for carrying me even when I didn't realize you were with me. I come to you with the deepest parts of me, things I don't remember, but things you saw firsthand. I am asking you to heal the imprints of my heart, making it possible for my beliefs to be in line with your truth about me. Enable me to attach in healthy ways to other people and to become the secure woman you created me to be. I am grateful for your love, your desire to be involved in my life, and your ability to turn any negative imprint into a new, beautifully healed Godprint. Amen.

4

every woman
can live a better story

*Of one thing I am perfectly sure:
God's story never ends with "ashes."*

ELISABETH ELLIOT

ARE YOU STILL PROCESSING how you answered the momplications assessment or figuring out how your mother imprinted
you? We've posed a lot of questions and given you a lot of
information to think about in the previous two chapters.
And yet we believe that if you put in the time for this self-
evaluation, you will reap lasting benefits.

We are still on our journeys. We can look back and see the
many ways God has healed us, and we can look forward and
see we still have a long way to go. Through our relationships
with God, both of us are finding what we were lacking from
our mothers.

Here are the assessment questions that made us think

long and hard. For me (Joan), one question that jumped out was "Has your mother seemed like a defeated victim of life rather than a victor?" When our family experienced several huge losses, I longed for my mother to show me how to be victorious over that pain. I longed for her to show me the way back to joy, for her to be the parent who could be bigger and stronger and take care of me emotionally. But she could not, so I was left to search for answers on my own.

I (Debbie) paused at the question "Have your interactions with your mother left you believing you are 'not enough'?" The words *not enough* have plagued my self-image for as long as I can remember. My mother never said those two words to me, but she spoke that message to my heart through her criticism and disinterest. It didn't seem as if I could do enough to get her acceptance or earn her love. I longed for a mother who made me feel special and celebrated, or at the very least a mother who noticed my efforts to please her.

A light in the darkness of my childhood was being enrolled in singing and dancing classes. Both of my parents agreed I had talent, and they enjoyed attending my performances at local venues in Los Angeles about two weekends a month. Those weekends were the best. They were the only times my mother seemed remotely pleased. She even smiled at me, fussing with my costume and hair. I treasured her attentiveness on those nights and lived for her applause. I also loved that Daddy wasn't sitting in a bar—he was there in the audience next to my mom. They appeared happy and seemed proud that I was their daughter. On the way home, we'd stop at a Big Boy restaurant for hot fudge sundaes. Those were good nights.

But off the stage, life was very different. I didn't get much attention from my mom, and Daddy wasn't around often, but I found that performance helped me cope with that unmet need. I became an overachiever and people pleaser. Whether it was completing my mom's list of household chores, getting good grades, or singing on the stage, every achievement seemed to keep the pain and insecurity in my heart from consuming me.

In my senior year of high school, I was surprised to be one of five senior girls chosen for the homecoming court. Mom wasn't interested in helping me pick out a dress, but she gave me her credit card to purchase one. I drove to the local mall and found a beautiful maroon dress. When I got home, I hung it in my room like a decoration, in anticipation of the big homecoming game.

The Friday night finally came, and as I sat on the back of a convertible heading onto the football field, I was giddy with excitement. I searched the stands for my parents and saw they were both there. *Perfect.* My escort, a tall and handsome classmate, led me up onto the platform where the others on the homecoming court waited for the reveal and crowning of Aviation High School's homecoming queen. I didn't have any expectations. Just knowing my parents were there was enough for me.

Then it happened. My name was blasted over the speakers, the sparkly tiara was placed on my head, and all I could think of was my mom in the stands. *She is finally going to be happy and excited for me.* Forget my peers—my heart yearned for her attention. I couldn't wait to get home from the dance to show her my crown and experience her approval.

Mom was asleep when I got home, so I placed my crown on my nightstand and went to bed with a smile on my face. What a day! The next morning, I bounded out of bed, grabbed my crown, and headed to the kitchen, where she was drinking coffee and reading the paper.

"Mom, look. I'm the queen!" I twirled around gleefully.

She looked up, set down her coffee cup, and said flatly, "They must have miscounted the votes."

I could barely breathe. Without a word, I walked out of the room—crushed beyond belief. I knew then what I had always suspected: I would never be enough for my mother.

Any belief that I was a person of worth died inside me that day. My own mother didn't like me, and given the chance, she wouldn't vote for me. Something had to be terribly wrong with me. The insecurity and fear that had been building for years became firmly rooted in my heart and mind.

MINDLESS THINKING

Scientists have discovered that when we are not engaged in a mental task, our brains return to a "default network." This is the state we are in when we are not thinking about anything in particular. Our imaginations can flow freely, filled with stories we tell ourselves about life, God, our expectations, and our identities. Some of the things we tell ourselves are true, and some are not.

After homecoming night, Debbie's default network became more negative. There is power in the identities we have assigned to ourselves. Dr. David Eckman said it well: "Identity is that picture we have of ourselves that has been painted across our hearts by our parents, our life experiences, and our culture. The picture determines how I view myself, the world, and God."[1]

Default thoughts usually happen unconsciously.

Becca was driving to meet two friends for lunch. The radio was on, but she wasn't paying attention to it. Instead, her mother's critical voice was inside her head, prompting Becca's own inner critic. "This outfit is ugly. These pants are getting tight and my stomach is pooching out. I'm disgusting. I wish I were tall and thin like Kristi. She looked amazing in those jeans she had on last time I saw her. Robin, not so much. She really needs to do something about that bush of frizzy hair, and she needs to lose weight."

Becca pulled her shirt down to hide her bulge. "Maybe I should tell Kristi and Robin I can't make it today. I will be humiliated if people see me." She imagined people in the restaurant whispering about her unattractiveness, just as her mother had done, saying things like "Look at the woman over there.

Someone should tell her how huge she looks in those pants." She began to mentally write texts to Kristi and Robin.

"All of a sudden not feeling well."

"Sorry. Something has come up and I can't make it."

She pictured their faces when they read her texts and heard them say with contempt, "Becca is such an ugly loser. I'm glad she's not coming." In a matter of minutes, Becca was overcome by loneliness and sadness descending over her like a cloud.

These thoughts and beliefs swirl in our minds, affecting us deeply. Becca's friends actually enjoyed her company and thought she was quite attractive. However, Becca had heard her mother criticizing herself and other women so often that she had internalized that critical voice. It had become part of Becca's default network.

YOUR PERSONAL DEFAULT NETWORK

All of us have a default network. What we think impacts how we live for God. However, here's the good news! Our minds can be renewed.

Don't copy the behavior and customs of this world, but let God transform you into a new person by changing the way you think. Then you will learn to know God's will for you, which is good and pleasing and perfect.

ROMANS 12:2

We all have a pattern of thinking that has been developed over the years from a variety of sources, including our family members, culture, schools, friends, etc. If you are told you are loved, you will probably believe you are loved. If you are criticized, there is a good chance you will become critical. If you are told you can't do something, you may never try. If you are treated like a princess, you most likely will become entitled. If you are ignored and uncared for, you may begin to believe you are worthless. If you are told that the world is a scary place, you will tend to be fearful. If you are lied to about other people and believe the lies, you may become distrustful. If you are lied to about yourself, you may gravitate toward shame or self-doubt. You get the idea. The ways our individual mind-sets have been formed are as unique as we are, but the beauty is that God knows us, even in the deepest recesses of our minds.

Freedom in Christ means speaking truth to ourselves. Any emotional ground our momplications have taken can be reclaimed, and any pattern of thinking that is hurting us can be turned around as our minds are renewed with truth.

Let the Spirit renew your thoughts and attitudes.

EPHESIANS 4:23

How can we begin to renew our minds and be liberated from the lies that have a grip on us?

- *Start by praying for God to give you greater awareness of your thoughts and build into your life the discipline of self-examination.*
- *Change your daydreams into mindful awareness. Pay attention to your thoughts.*
- *Ask yourself if your thoughts are true. Are they in line with what the Bible teaches about God, about others, about yourself and your destiny?*
- *When you recognize faulty thinking, refocus your thoughts on what is true (see Philippians 4:8) as a way to "take captive every thought to make it obedient to Christ" (2 Corinthians 10:5, NIV).*

GOD WORKS IN UNEXPECTED WAYS

When my (Joan's) father died, a huge negative shift took place in my default network. My habitual way of seeing myself as safe and cared for changed to a new habitual way of thinking. I began to believe that I was abandoned and alone.

On the night after finding out about his death, I wanted to know what had happened to him. Where was he? Was it possible that he no longer existed? Would I ever see him again? I had frequently attended a Catholic church with my friend Nancy, and through her and other friends I had been exposed to the idea of heaven. Was it possible my dad might be there with God? I hoped so. So I tried an experiment.

I looked up at my bedroom ceiling and said, "God, if you are real, and if my dad is with you, I want you to prove it to me by moving this pencil while I sleep." I picked up the pencil on my dresser and carefully placed it exactly parallel to my bed. If God moved it, I would know.

The next morning the pencil was exactly as I had left it. Furious, I lashed out at God: "Either you don't exist or you don't care about me, so I'm NOT GOING TO BELIEVE IN YOU." And for the next twenty-one years, I didn't.

I did my best to find meaning and joy in life, but under all my activity I felt desperately empty and purposeless. I went to New York for college, then moved to San Francisco. I dated, enjoyed friends, traveled, and achieved academic and career success. But the ache inside me remained. I longed for assurance that someone was watching over me, caring for me, and guiding me. I couldn't shake the sense that I was all alone in the world. *Is there a point to my life? If we just live and then die and there is nothing more, why are we here?*

I explored self-help workshops, Hinduism, Buddhism, ascended masters, swamis, gurus—anything that might give me answers. Some of them helped or gave me hope for a time, but nothing lasted.

Shortly after my thirtieth birthday, I was in my hometown for the weekend to attend a wedding. Late that evening, I went with a group of other wedding guests to a hole-in-the-wall bar. As we sat laughing and talking, the bartender came up to our group and said, "Are any of you Joan?" Surprised, I identified myself, and he told me I had a telephone call.

"Hello?"

"Hi, Joanie! It's Diane!" I was dumbfounded. As a little girl, Diane would often come to my house to find refuge from her own imperfect family. It was a short walk from her house to ours, and she spent almost all her free time with us. She was like another sister to me.

"How in the world did you know I was in town? How did you know I was at this bar?" I was awed by the unlikeliness of her phone call.

"I'm in town to visit my mom. I ran into your mom at the grocery store tonight, and she told me where you were."

An hour later Diane and I were sitting in low lawn chairs behind my childhood home, our bare feet in the grass. My mother was asleep in the house, and the warm, humid night was quiet.

We eagerly caught up on each other's news, and then, as our conversation slowed, Diane said, "I've become a Christian."

Diane? A Christian? Diane was smart. She was a doctor. She was scientific. How could she believe in some mythical God who sat up in the clouds? It did not compute.

"How did this happen? What do you believe?" One question led to another, and she answered each one honestly, humbly, and authentically.

I don't remember most of what she said to me. I do know that after that night I still had very little understanding of the basic doctrines of the Christian faith. She never pressed me or invited me to pray. She only answered my questions.

Although I don't remember the content of our conversation, I do very vividly remember Jesus becoming real to me that night. I couldn't see him with my physical eyes, but I could envision the love in his eyes. I couldn't touch him with my hands, but I could feel his strong, safe presence. I knew I didn't have to do anything or be anything other than who I was to be loved by him. Something in me said yes to him that night.

The next day I went back to California. Slowly, from the inside out, the relationship I had started with Christ began to change me. Activities that had previously appealed to me no longer interested me. Christian people began to appear in my life—people that I actually liked and respected. For the first time, I read the Bible, and after a few years, I even went to a church. More and more I viewed myself and my world through new eyes. A positive shift was taking place in my default network.

I am not alone. I am loved. I am safe. I have been chosen and adopted into an eternal family. My life has value and purpose.

WE ARE PART OF A BIGGER STORY

God's story is one of salvation, reconciliation, and healing. We both have found peace by looking beyond what we learned from our mothers, beyond the "sad story" to the story God tells. That's where we all need to begin. Take a moment and read these truths about how important you are to God:

> You saw me before I was born.
>> Every day of my life was recorded in your book.
> Every moment was laid out
>> before a single day had passed.
> PSALM 139:16

> In him we live and move and have our being.
> ACTS 17:28, NIV

> We are God's masterpiece. He has created us anew
> in Christ Jesus, so we can do the good things he
> planned for us long ago.
> EPHESIANS 2:10

As we examine things in our lives that need God's touch, it's important that we remember God never changes, always loves us, rescues us, and restores us to his original design—naked and unashamed. What does that mean? It means we are free to walk with God without pretense. Free to be imperfect mothers and imperfect daughters who are works in progress. Free to have flaws and problems between us. Free to receive healing and wholeness and be comfortable with who we are and who God is. Free to extend grace to ourselves when we receive God's grace.

GOD OFFERS FRESH MEANING
TO OUR STORIES

Is your mother-daughter story starting to take shape at all? Are some things falling more into place for you, and other things that seemed terribly important fading away? That's how God begins to change our stories. Our lives are made up of an endless series of experiences, but the meaning we assign to them changes over time. At one time, the stars in the night sky may have been considered just scattered points of light, but then people connected the dots and saw shapes that they named—a giant dipper with a bowl and handle, and a hunter with a sword hanging from his belt. In the same way, we connect the dots of our experiences when we give them meaning.

Research shows that "the meaning of significant emotional events develops over time as individuals reflect on the story's personal importance as well as share the story with others to glean their reactions."[2] For example, Debbie saw how her mother treated her and assigned the meaning "There is something wrong with me." But when Debbie adds God's truth to her interpretation, she can say, "Though I was affected by my mother wounds, God has always loved me. I am his, and I am enough in him." The facts of our stories don't change, but the meaning we take from our stories—the overarching conclusions we draw—certainly can.

God is referred to as "Father" throughout the Bible, rather than "Mother," but he displays all the traits of a perfect parent—male or female. As we grow in our intimacy with him, he can fill in what may have been lacking in our relationships with our mothers. Read the following descriptions of God and the accompanying Scriptures, letting their truth touch you deeply:

- He is present and available. *"Where can I go from your Spirit? Where can I flee from your presence?"* *(Psalm 139:7, NIV); "I will never leave you nor forsake you" (Hebrews 13:5, ESV).*
- He celebrates us with music. *"He will rejoice over you with joyful songs" (Zephaniah 3:17).*
- He comforts us. *"God is our merciful Father and the source of all comfort. He comforts us in all our troubles so that we can comfort others" (2 Corinthians 1:3-4).*
- He is trustworthy and true to his word. *"All of God's promises have been fulfilled in Christ with a resounding 'Yes!'" (2 Corinthians 1:20).*
- He encourages us, blesses us, and sends us out to be fruitful, fully using the gifts and talents we have been given to serve others. *"There are different kinds of spiritual gifts, but the same Spirit is the source of them all. There are different kinds of service, but we serve the same Lord. God works in different ways, but it is the same God who does the work in all of us. A spiritual gift is given to each of us so we can help each other" (1 Corinthians 12:4-7).*
- He teaches us what is true and right. *"All Scripture is inspired by God and is useful to teach us what is true and*

to make us realize what is wrong in our lives. It corrects us when we are wrong and teaches us to do what is right" (2 Timothy 3:16).

- He always wants what is best for us, even if it is painful to us in the short term. *"God causes everything to work together for the good of those who love God and are called according to his purpose for them" (Romans 8:28).*
- He loves us so much that he died for us. *"God showed his great love for us by sending Christ to die for us while we were still sinners" (Romans 5:8).*

A NEW ENGRAVING

We are both spirit and flesh (i.e., human beings). It is important for us to recognize this. Why? Because we often live according to the patterns and imprints of our human experiences. That is where our wounds, our false beliefs, our attachment styles, and our default networks reside. When we are born again, something beautiful and life-changing happens. We become new creations, reborn by the Holy Spirit. We are free.

Flesh gives birth to flesh, but the Spirit gives birth to spirit.

JOHN 3:6, NIV

If anyone is in Christ, the new creation has come; the old has gone, the new is here!

2 CORINTHIANS 5:17, NIV

This newness of life happens on the inside when the Holy Spirit indwells us. We can start living in the power of God's Spirit rather than from our humanness. God begins to break the faulty patterns we have used for protection, and He restores our hearts, minds, emotions, and personalities. Are you ready to start living anew by the Spirit? Your life will never be the same.

Explore Your Story

1. Reread the story about your mother that you wrote at the end of chapter 1, reminding yourself that God wants to replace the lies you have believed with his truth. When that happens, the hold the lies have on you will be broken, and God's presence will fill any empty places in your life.

2. Revise your story by placing it in God's bigger story. Reflect on your past and consider where you have seen God's healing hand. Look to your future and express your hope and faith in a God who loves you more than you can imagine. Remind yourself that your story isn't over yet.

3. List things that you recognize as your default thinking patterns. Identify how some of the ways you frame your circumstances might be keeping you from freedom.

4. Read Galatians 5:16-26. What are the differences between the Spirit-led life and the human patterns ingrained in you? Remember, the goal is not to blame your parents. When you identify the negative patterns that control you, you can take them to Jesus and let his Spirit heal you for his purpose and glory.

Connect with God

Powerful and trustworthy Father, I thank you that you are above all things. You have placed your Holy Spirit within me, and I ask you to change me by the power of your Spirit. I desire freedom, and I know you desire it for me too. Help me believe in the bigger story by aligning my thoughts with the truth of your love and care for me. Right now, my past is my frame of reference, but I want your truth to be my reference point going forward. May I accept my past as part of my story but recognize that the story is not over. You redeem every part of it by the power of your love and grace toward me. Amen.

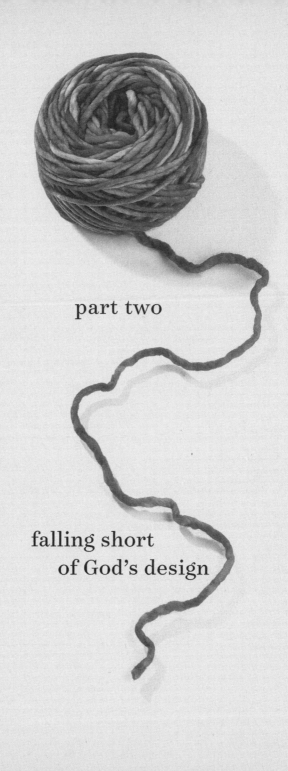

part two

falling short
of God's design

Old childhood issues always surface during times
of stress and pressure. I've known plenty of people
who were pretty good at holding everything
together until life's challenges snuck up on them
and kicked the foundation out from under
them. . . . "Wounds that are not dealt with
sit and fester within us until they eventually
spew their venom onto those we love and care
about. But wounds that are healed can become
a source of great inspiration and wisdom."

RICK JOHNSON

5

mom, where are you?

I will never leave you nor forsake you.

HEBREWS 13:5, ESV

NEEDS.

We all have them—some fulfilled and others still waiting to be.

In part 2 (chapters 5 through 8), we will look at four basic needs a daughter has in her relationship with her mother and what happens if a need is unmet. How did we come up with these four needs? In many books about mothers, each chapter is about a type of mother—the narcissistic mother, the addicted mother, and the depressed mother, to name a few examples.

We are taking a different approach, focusing less on labels for our mothers and more on what we as daughters may have lacked in this important relationship. This helps us avoid getting caught up in our mothers' mistakes and helps refocus our energy on positive steps we can take toward healing. When we identify the unmet needs in ourselves, we can ask God to help fill in the gaps. There are countless ways we could have categorized the needs of daughters, and many stories fit in multiple categories. However, we have pinpointed these four needs to help you begin your journey toward wholeness:

- *Daughters need a present, attuned, nurturing mother (chapter 5).*
- *Daughters need to feel safe (chapter 6).*
- *Daughters need teaching and guidance (chapter 7).*
- *Daughters need to be celebrated for the unique persons God has made them to be (chapter 8).*

A daughter's most important needs from her mother evolve over time. In the early years, she needs her mother to be present, attuned, and protective. In her school years, she needs her mother to teach and guide her. When a daughter becomes an adult, she needs her mother to let go and celebrate her as the unique person God has made her to be. However, all these needs are essential and are present in some form at all stages of life.

As you read through these chapters, we pray that the concepts and stories will open your eyes to your own unmet needs. Some experiences may have seemed normal to you as you grew up but left lasting imprints that continue to trigger your emotions and adversely affect your relationships today. There will be times when you do not relate at all to the stories in these chapters, and there will be times when you do. Be open to what God wants to show you.

WHY PRESENCE AND ATTUNEMENT MATTER

Are you familiar with the classic picture book *The Runaway Bunny?* An adventurous baby bunny engages his mother in an imaginary "what-if" game of hide-and-seek, seeing to what lengths she would go to find and be with him. As the baby bunny soon learns, there are no barriers or restrictions for his mother. Nothing can prevent her from being there for him. All for one reason—"You are my little bunny."[1]

The story illustrates what every child (for our book, every daughter) needs to know—that no matter where she goes or what she does or how she tests her mother's limits, her mother's presence will be a constant that she can depend on. That reassurance calms her and gives her a sense of safety. The child doesn't have to face the world alone. Her mother will be there to care for her. It sends the message that the child is important and valued, that she is worth her mother's time and attention. It gives her confidence to venture out and explore her world.

In the children's story, the baby bunny and his mother are "in tune" with each other. There is a playful, creative interaction between them, as if they are making music together. That attunement requires more than a mother's physical presence; a child needs an emotionally present mother, a mother who "gets" her. She needs a mother whose brain is in tune with her brain like a guitar string with a tuner.

The most critical time for a daughter to have a physically and emotionally present mother is her early years. Obviously, an infant depends on her mother for survival, to feed and care for her. However, infants need more than food and diaper changes. Studies have shown that infants living in crowded, understaffed orphanages, even with all their basic physical needs met, do not thrive if they are not touched, held, and given eye-to-eye interaction.

Eye-to-eye interaction is a key component of attunement. When a mother looks into the eyes of her baby, she is literally shaping her child's brain. The mother's facial expressions, the light in her eyes, and her soothing words impact the child's less-developed brain, teaching her to modulate the ups and downs of her emotions and return to a state of well-being. A mother's attuned presence at this stage also lays the foundation for the child's attachment style. If the mother is consistently there for her daughter, the daughter will begin to develop a secure attachment style.

If you are a young mom, the best gift you can give your child is to learn to regulate your own emotions. If you struggle with depression or anxiety (something many mothers experience), get the help you need. You cannot help your child regulate her strong emotions if you cannot regulate your own. She looks to you to use your adult capacity to return her to a state of calm.

You may not know if or how much your mother was there for you when you were a baby. Parts of your brain that store memories were still developing then. Trust God to reveal the truth to you through recaptured memories or in stories from adults who were there in your early years. Why is it important to ask God about events from so long ago? Because these years of earliest and deepest imprinting provide understanding of who we are now.

THE IMPORTANCE OF ATTUNEMENT

The summer after my brother died, I (Joan) walked into our house with a friend and found my distraught mother on her knees next to our vacuum cleaner. She said the vacuum cleaner had broken and she was trying to fix it. Not wanting anything else to be broken in our lives, I said, "Why don't you just buy a new one?"

She looked at me as if I had slapped her. "We don't have the money."

Tears filled her eyes, and she crumpled to the floor moaning, "I don't want to live."

My friend and I stood frozen.

She lifted her head, looked at us, and said, "Get out! Get out of the house now."

I was horrified and terrified, but she was so wrapped up in her own pain, she couldn't see mine. She wasn't emotionally present or attuned to me, so she couldn't comfort me, and I felt completely alone.

Thankfully, most mothers are doing the best they can to love their daughters. Sometimes mothers make selfish choices; however, most mothers who are not attuned are like Joan's mom, women dealing with emotions or circumstances beyond their control that make them unable to give their daughters what they need. Here are some reasons why a mother may not be present and attuned to her daughter:

- *death*
- *depression or anxiety*
- *other mental illnesses*
- *physical illness (being in pain, bedridden, or hospitalized)*
- *grief*
- *addiction (alcoholism, drugs, work, gaming, sex, relationships)*
- *immaturity (having a child before she is mature or responsible enough)*
- *lack of support (overwhelmed by the responsibilities of life and child-rearing)*
- *lack of resources (inability to provide good childcare while she is away)*
- *unresolved trauma (car accident, rape, betrayal, or divorce)*
- *focus on another loved one who is ill or needy*

- *preoccupation with a difficult relationship (or inability to say no to others)*
- *involvement in an abusive relationship*
- *having a distant mother herself (and therefore not having the skills of attunement)*
- *having an unwanted pregnancy and not wanting to be a mother to her child*

As adults we can face the reality that we have been wounded, while also developing grace and understanding for our mothers because of the circumstances they faced. This is helpful because it unravels our belief that we deserved to be abandoned.

Just as there are many reasons why a mother might be unavailable, there are also many ways in which a daughter can be affected. Here is an overview:

- *feeling alone in the world—a painful sense of disconnection*
- *believing she does not belong*
- *anxiety or hypervigilance—a sense that the world is not a safe place*
- *depression or lack of joy*
- *being overly emotional*
- *extreme neediness*
- *emotional frozenness*
- *anger issues*
- *extreme self-reliance*

- *reduced sense of self (lack of awareness of her own emotions, likes, and dislikes)*
- *lack of self-esteem*
- *limited confidence in being a woman*
- *eating disorders*
- *addiction to alcohol or other substances*
- *sex or relationship addiction*
- *workaholism*
- *perfectionism*
- *inability to remember childhood*

This is a varied list, and these symptoms can result from things other than mother wounds (we don't want to blame our mothers for everything). Read it lightly, noting to yourself which traits you may have. You are slowly forming a picture—an understanding of the shape of your wounding and how God wants to heal and fill in your empty places.

The following stories illustrate three common types of fallout of not having an attuned and present mother: a sense of not belonging, lack of joy, and vulnerability to addictive relationships.

"I Don't Belong"

Shelly is a fun-loving young woman who considers her mother to be one of the most impressive women she has ever known. The two never argue or bicker over anything.

On the surface, their relationship looks healthy. But Shelly's story with her mother plays out differently in the deepest part of her soul. Not only did she and her mother not make "music" together, Shelly doesn't remember them ever having much of a connection.

As Shelly grew up and began to study personality styles and temperaments, she realized there was a clear reason for the disconnect. She and her mother were nothing alike. One was a thinker, the other a feeler. One was an introvert, the other an extrovert. While her mother connected seamlessly with her other children, who were more like her, she didn't connect with Shelly. Though physically present to Shelly, she was not attuned to what was happening in Shelly's heart and soul.

While this disconnection was unintentional on her mother's part, Shelly's self-esteem suffered. She grew up with a deep insecurity that she was somehow not okay at her core. In addition, since she didn't feel as if she connected to anyone in the family, she developed a belief that said, "I don't belong." That early imprint was pressed upon her over and over as she grew up.

Even though she is deeply devoted to her family, Shelly still feels as if she doesn't belong and is alone when they are all together. A lack of belonging has created a sense of insecurity in her that affects relationships with friends and coworkers. As she has gotten older, Shelly has become hypersensitive to being left out or forgotten. If someone overlooks her, her emotions spiral, changing her from happy to harried in minutes. Social media has become a trigger that amps up her insecurity. A simple post "proves" that she has been left out, tapping into her past pain.

Can you relate to similar feelings of emptiness or not belonging? Perhaps you have always longed for love and thought for some reason you did not deserve to receive that love. Children who did not have a present or attuned mother are wounded. Like Shelly, a certain trigger may unexpectedly unravel us emotionally. Instead of growing older gracefully, we may find ourselves becoming more reactive and bitter.

A mother cannot be faulted for being nothing like her child. However, as the child grows, it can be hard for the mother to relate or connect to someone so different from her. Because of that discomfort, the mother may unconsciously withhold her presence or attunement, leaving the daughter to wonder why. Often the daughter concludes that her mother must not like her, and that if that is the case, there must be something considerably wrong with her.

"I Have No Joy"

Mary's mother was an alcoholic and completely self-absorbed. During her alcoholic rages, she would become verbally abusive, telling Mary she never wanted her and calling her "stupid" and "ugly." Mary's mother would rarely prepare food, bathe her, or comb her daughter's hair. She treated her like an inconvenience.

When Mary grew up, she married a man who treated

her with indifference. His emotional unavailability seemed normal to her. We are often drawn to romantic partners who recreate the dysfunction of our childhoods.

When Mary received a diagnosis of cancer, her husband became angry and even colder toward her. She longed for him to love and nurture her just as she had always longed for her mother to love and nurture her, yet both have always been dry wells. Mary describes being in constant "psychic pain." This dull emotional pain makes Mary unable to feel or experience joy. Growing up, she questioned her mother's love, and now she questions her husband's love. Being treated with indifference has left a large void in Mary's heart.

Research shows that our capacity for joy is built through connection. Psychic pain occurs when there is disconnection and loneliness. We connect when people are emotionally present and attuned to us, which Mary's mother and husband were not. Mary never experienced the joyful interaction that the mother bunny and her little bunny did.

"I Long for Love"

If a daughter's first need for her mother's love is not met, the emptiness and craving left in her core may drive her to look to others to fill that need. For some women, the craving is for men. For others, women may appear to satisfy their deep longings. These relationships may be sexual or they may not.

Julia did not identify as gay, but she began a relationship with Barbara because she liked being close to her. Barbara made her feel like the most important person in the world. "I felt like the center of the universe, safe, cared for, like everything was going to be okay."

Julia is an educated, successful individual. She could see that Barbara was self-centered, controlling, and toxic for her, yet she could not seem to pull away. They bought a house together, and as their lives became entangled, Julia lost herself more and more. It took her eight years to move out, yet even then Barbara still had a magnetic pull on her. Reflecting on all of it, Julia said, "She meets some deep need in me that I cannot describe. Now I am engaged to marry Sam, but when she calls or e-mails me, I still feel an intense longing for the way she could make me feel."

Kelly McDaniel, a therapist who specializes in female love and sex addiction, observed,

Addictive relationships are a desperate, consuming attempt to find love. In the work I do as a therapist, I'm reminded daily of the painful legacy for women who didn't have a healthy bond with their mothers. When early attachment doesn't happen, a daughter essentially loses her first opportunity for love. This loss is devastating and has ripple effects throughout her life. Using sex and romance to fill the emptiness inside is the unconscious attempt to heal this primal wound.[2]

SUBSTITUTE MOTHERS

Many of us have had other women step into our lives and fill us with love and good things. Did you have a grandmother, aunt, older sister, or family friend who was there for you? Thankfully, every ounce of love deposited into us was needed and made us stronger in ways we probably don't even realize. Still, despite the love of others, our little-girl hearts often long for our own mothers' love.

In my (Debbie's) earliest years, much of my mother's angst toward me was covered by my sister's love. I adored Sharon, my only sibling, who was a teenager when I was born. I secretly wished she could be my mother. She was beautiful, kind, loving, and interested in me. Mom seemed to like her, and I thought if I could be more like my sister, then Mom would like me, too.

By the time I was in the first grade, the person dearest to me was married. Although Sharon was busy starting her own life and family, Mom relied on her to care for me, shop for me, and fill in when Mom was not there. I can't imagine who I would be today if I hadn't had the love of my sister.

But as much as I loved Sharon and she loved me, when I was dropped off at her house, I realized I wasn't an intimate part of her family. I was the outsider who watched in awe as she nurtured and loved her little ones. It was different from anything I experienced at home. I longed for the kind of motherly love—the attunement—she gave her children. Certainly, I wasn't getting attunement from my mother, and Sharon couldn't fill the void.

For a long time, I didn't realize the lasting impact of three beliefs I'd carried with me since I was young—beliefs that I didn't deserve to be loved, that I could never be enough, and that I didn't belong. These negative imprints had been pressed down and cemented in my heart. I knew I struggled with thinking I was not enough, but I never saw that these beliefs all came from the same wound. When added together, these negative beliefs were like dynamite, destroying the good that my sister tried to deposit in my life.

I still struggle with feeling left out when I am not invited to an event or included in a group. But now, as the Debbie who is learning her triggers and receiving healing from God, I can ask myself, *Is this a legitimate concern, or is it just little Debbie?* Most of the time, that is enough to help me stop and whisper a prayer: "Jesus, help me to live as the grown-up woman I am today and not in the hurts of little Debbie. Thank you for helping me understand that I have what I need because I belong to you."

Perhaps you were blessed to have a woman who was not your biological mother step into the mother role in your life. Or maybe it was several women. Even though you may have been loved generously, can you identify a longing for something more? The truth is, we all have holes in our hearts that only God can fill.

TRUE ATTUNEMENT WITH GOD

If you believe you missed out on motherly presence and attunement, God offers a healing imprint—a "Godprint." He promises that he is constantly there for us even when our infantile spiritual awareness does not fully grasp it. His nature is to nourish and sustain us, much as a mother nourishes and sustains an infant at her breast. One of God's names is El Roi (see Genesis 16:13)—the God who sees us. Like a good mother, he is always watching over those who are his, listening for our cries (see Psalm 34:15). He lavishes us with unending love and delights in us. He is the source of our joy.

David's words in Psalm 139 confirm that we have a parent who is constantly with us:

> I can never escape from your Spirit!
> I can never get away from your presence!
> If I go up to heaven, you are there;
>   if I go down to the grave, you are there.
> If I ride the wings of the morning,
>   if I dwell by the farthest oceans,
> even there your hand will guide me,
>   and your strength will support me.
> PSALM 139:7-10

We cannot expect other people to provide our soul care. People can forget or even leave us, but God will always be present. The prophet Isaiah proclaimed the future sign that

God would come to dwell among us, which would be ful-filled in Jesus' birth:

> They will call him Immanuel, which means "God is
> with us."
>
> MATTHEW 1:23

During his life on earth, Jesus interacted with people, walked and talked with them, related to them, and offered them healing, direction, and hope. That is still true for us today. God is always with us! No matter what the details of our pasts, no matter what our stories tell us to the contrary, when we truly believe that God is present, we will begin to experience a deep sense of being treasured. When we try to hide or run away from God, he pulls us back to himself over and over again. He is attuned to us because he loves us. Knowing he is there and accessible provides us with incomparable strength.

> Be strong and courageous. Do not be afraid or terrified
> because of them, for the LORD your God goes with
> you; he will never leave you nor forsake you.
>
> DEUTERONOMY 31:6, NIV

Before he returned to the Father, Jesus promised his disciples,

> I will ask the Father, and he will give you another
> advocate to help you and be with you forever—the

Spirit of truth. . . . He lives with you and will be in you. I will not leave you as orphans.

JOHN 14:16-18, NIV

That promise still holds true. Often girls who do not feel connected to their mothers feel like emotional orphans. They grow up with a set of false conclusions about themselves that become a fixed mind-set of lies:

- *God doesn't love me.*
- *I am not worthy to receive anything from God.*
- *I don't belong in my family.*
- *No one cares about me.*
- *My feelings don't matter.*
- *There is no such thing as a happy family.*
- *The best way to avoid hurt is to isolate myself from others.*
- *Significant people in my life will not be there for me when I need help.*
- *I am valuable to others only for what I can do for them.*
- *Even when I give my best, it is not good enough.*

These lies are powerful, but we don't have to surrender to them. Remember that God promises not to leave us as orphans. His Word says we are loved by him, adopted into his family, and wanted by him.

I will be your Father, and you will be my sons and daughters.

2 CORINTHIANS 6:18

God decided in advance to adopt us into his own family by bringing us to himself through Jesus Christ. This is what he wanted to do, and it gave him great pleasure.

EPHESIANS 1:5

Whether our mothers are alive or have passed away, there is hope for those who have grown up with an orphan spirit. If you are a follower of Christ, the Holy Spirit lives in you forever—to counsel, direct, and protect.

Perhaps the message that God is with you and you are never alone is just words on paper for you, a thought that others express as spiritual truth. But what if this truth could change everything? What if you embraced this one truth? Could it be that God's presence could heal you, deliver you, and help you no longer feel alone?

Explore Your Story

1. Find a copy of *The Runaway Bunny* at the library or a bookstore. As you read it, what emotions does the story evoke in you? Did your mother respond to the music of your heart? Was there joy between the two of you? Did you feel connection and belonging? Did you feel treasured?

2. If you felt alone, prayerfully journal the story of why you felt that way. What messages were pressed into your soul

as a child? Were there times when you felt like an orphan? This may take a while, but sit with it and let God illuminate the parts of your story that need healing.

3. How do those imprinted messages continue to affect you today?

4. What other mother figures stepped in for you? How did their presence affect you?

5. What truths about God's presence speak to you? Why do these truths stand out?

Connect with God

Lord, thank you for your presence. Though I haven't always known it or felt it, you have promised to always be with me. I come to you with every moment that I have felt alone and the lasting effects that feeling has had on me. Please remove the fear, disconnection, and insecurity from my heart. I am grateful to be your child who belongs to you and receives your love. I invite you to re-parent me. Open up my heart so healing can take place. I desire to be true to who you have made me to be. Although my relationship with my mother may have wounded me, I believe both of us are deeply loved by you. Thank you for offering me healing. Amen.

6

mom, will you keep me safe?

You, O L ORD, are a shield around me.

PSALM 3:3

I T WAS A DREARY S EPTEMBER NIGHT in the California beach town where I (Debbie) grew up. My dad was more than three hours late from work, and my mother was fuming, sick of his antics. Occasionally on the Fridays my dad got paid, he would stop at a bar rather than come straight home. After dinner, I sat on the sofa, my stomach churning from my mother's anger, and stared at the front door, waiting for my dad.

I finally went to bed, hoping he was okay and this would all blow over. But before long, my mom woke me up.

"Get up and get dressed. We're going to go find your father." After I threw on some clothes and a jacket, Mom and I got in the car and began to search for Daddy. It seemed like forever, going in and out of parking lots all over town. Finally, Mom spotted Dad's car and pulled over. She looked at me. "Go inside and find your father, and don't come out without him!"

"Mom, I'm afraid. I don't know what it's like in there. What if Daddy doesn't want to leave? Please don't make me do this."

"Don't argue with me. Get out of the car. Now!"

My heart raced as I pulled on the bar's heavy door. I could barely see anything at first because it was so dark inside. The stench of beer and the cloud of smoke nearly choked me. As I entered, heads turned and I heard one man say, "Are you lost, little girl?" which drew laughs around the room.

Finally, my eyes adjusted to the dim room and I spotted my dad at the bar, perched on a stool. I went up to him, tugged at his sleeve, and said quietly, "Dad, we need to go home," but he stared at me blankly. He was so drunk he didn't recognize me.

Fortunately, the bartender came over, eased my dad off the stool, and supported him as my dad stumbled out to the car. I sheepishly thanked the bartender before I got into the back seat. Mom screamed at my dad for a few blocks before he finally passed out. I hated my father's drinking but was even more deathly afraid of how it made my mother react. When I was young, my world was dreadfully unsafe.

On another occasion my father came home late as usual after drinking.

"Daddy, where have you been? I have been waiting all night. You promised you were going to take me to

Woolworth's to get the holiday Barbie doll. Now it's too late; the store is about to close."

He had been promising to take me to get the doll all week. "Come on, get in the car," he said. "We'll get there before they close." I hopped in the front seat, and within a few minutes, I was terrified.

My intoxicated father wove the speeding car through the streets of Los Angeles, trying to get to the store across town. Forget honking horns or red lights—they didn't seem to matter to him. Why did my mother allow me to go with him? As I slid back and forth on the seat, I thought that night would be my last one on earth. Along with the doll, I received the very real and growing fear that I could not count on either of my parents to keep me safe.

Fear became a constant in my life, always present even when I was clearly secure.

Once the enemy of our souls plants a lie, the roots grow deep into the soil of our minds. For most of us, cutting off the branches of individual fears seems sufficient. But God's intention is to pull up the vine and get to the root of the lie, fear, and problem. That's when we can have true freedom, knowing that despite our circumstances, God is with us and we are safe.

THE NEED FOR PROTECTION

Children are vulnerable and dependent. They are not able to protect themselves, and they need the adults in their world to represent God's character by

- *being their safe place—their refuge*
- *comforting them and helping them calm down after a scary or traumatic incident*
- *watching over them and protecting them from dangerous circumstances and people*
- *teaching them to discern when it is appropriate and not appropriate to be afraid*

As I (Joan) heard Debbie's story, I realized how fortunate I was. I had not been put into those kinds of frightening situations growing up. Obviously, Debbie's father was not a safe, comforting presence when he was drunk, but Debbie's mother could have been her refuge, the person who helped her cope with her father's alcoholism. As I look through my therapist's lens, I ask, What could Debbie's mother have done differently?

She could have physically protected Debbie. She could have refrained from sending her into a bar late at night and refused to allow her to ride in a car driven by her intoxicated father.

She could have been her comforter. When Debbie was afraid or upset, her mother could have taken her into her arms and encouraged Debbie to tell her what she was feeling, validating and giving words to her emotions.

She could have taught Debbie the skills of self-regulation. If Debbie's mom had been able to regulate herself—

*acknowledging her own feelings but not letting them
take over—she could have calmed Debbie and taught
her to regulate all her terrifying emotions.*

*Even when Debbie's mother lost control (which happens to
all of us), she could have come back later to apologize and
discuss how upsetting the incident had been for both of
them. This would have helped Debbie return to a sense
of "all is well." Since this didn't happen, Debbie's young
nervous system became almost permanently hypervigilant,
like a gas pedal constantly pushed to the floor. Her
"normal" state was one of fear, not safety and calm.*

No one wants to see children grow up in an environment
plagued by fear, anger, or neglect. But mothering is a learned
skill. No woman is born knowing how to care for children,
though most mothers do the best they can. Sometimes they
make mistakes, or they may get thrown off track by circumstances beyond their control. Just as there are reasons why
a mother cannot always be present, there are explanations
for why a mother may not always provide protection and
safety. The good news is that children are resilient and do
not require perfection. It is natural for them to be fearful on
occasion as long as it isn't a constant way of life.

APPROPRIATE AND INAPPROPRIATE FEAR

The world can be dangerous, and we need a healthy dose of
caution in order to survive. The goal is to have *appropriate*

fear. Fear when one gets close to the edge of a steep cliff is appropriate. Fear of taking a shower is not. Ideally, as we mature, we learn to discern which situations and people are safe (both physically and emotionally) and which are not. We will be able to trust and open up to those who love us and want the best for us, but we will guard ourselves against those who might use or abuse us.

As we discussed in part 1, our early relationships and our attachment styles impact everything, including whether or not we are capable of appropriate fear. At the extreme, children raised in orphanages, without a present, attuned, comforting caretaker in their early months, often develop something called reactive attachment disorder (RAD). Either they refuse to allow anyone near them (i.e., they fear everyone and trust no one), or they will go to any stranger (i.e., they fear no one and trust everyone). Most of us are not scarred to such an extreme, but we may have tendencies in one or both directions:

> *We erect walls and don't let others in—we don't trust people when it would be appropriate to trust them.*
> *We lack healthy, self-protective boundaries—we trust others too easily or let them overstep our rights.*

Healthy attachment is not all or nothing; it includes wisdom, discernment, and appropriateness to the specific situation or person. It involves being in the present and not mired in our memories of past trauma. Our mothers have a huge impact on our development in this area.

When a child does not feel safe or is missing the protection she needs, this feeling can balloon into inappropriate fear. This lack of trust can manifest itself in any number of ways. Here are some of them:

- *anxiety disorders*
- *difficulty forming fulfilling, close relationships (which can lead to loneliness, a sense of not belonging, or depression)*
- *forming a false public self that protects her from vulnerability*
- *fear of commitment*
- *turning to alcohol/food/sex/work (something other than people) for comfort*
- *choosing controlling or abusive spouses*
- *becoming controlling or abusive*
- *inability to advocate or speak up for herself*
- *lack of confidence*
- *reluctance to take appropriate risks*

Do you see any of these manifestations in your story? How has your childhood relationship with your mom given you appropriate or inappropriate fear? Each of us has an individual and complex story of how we were (or were not) protected, how we were imprinted to feel safe or unsafe in the world and with others, and how we coped with our situations.

Your mother may have had a major or a minor role. Others may have stepped in to significantly help or hurt you.

THREE HARMFUL SITUATIONS

The specific events and memories of your life are unique to you, including the level of trauma you experienced. Nevertheless, it can be helpful to look at other mother-daughter stories for insight into your own story. Here are three common ways in which mothers may fall short of providing safety for their children. None of them will be your exact story, but some aspects may sound familiar.

1. Mom Is Abusive or Unpredictable

An abusive mother is one of the most confusing challenges a daughter can face. How can the person who carried you in her womb, who is supposed to love you, and whom you look to for your very survival be the one who hurts you so terribly? Unpredictable abuse is even more damaging. The child never knows which mommy will appear—nice mommy or mean mommy. She lives in a constant state of uncertainty and fear.

Physical abuse inflicts horrible wounds, but verbal abuse is also harmful. The marks that harsh, demeaning words make in a child's heart can last a lifetime. The playground rhyme "Sticks and stones may break my bones, but words will never hurt me" is simply untrue. Yes, physical assault hurts, but ugly words can break our hearts as children. We are left believing what was said to us: "You're no good. You're lazy. You don't know anything." In our early years we cannot bear the thought that our parents, the people we depend on for our survival, might be wrong. So we blame ourselves and adopt the viewpoint that we deserve the abuse—that we are fundamentally bad or flawed.

Why do mothers say harsh and demeaning things to their daughters? Some are just mean and lack empathy. Some thoughtlessly repeat words that were said to them when they were young. Many succumb to their emotions and speak from the immature and unhealed parts of themselves.

"I tried so hard to be good and not set my mother off," said Kim. "One minute she would be sweet, telling me she didn't feel well and asking me to make her a cup of tea. Then a minute later she would be a screaming witch, telling me she hated me and wished I had never been born. I usually didn't know what I had said or done to cause it. I just knew I must be pretty bad."

Not only the cruel words but the unpredictability of the outbursts made it hard for Kim to feel safe. She was always on high alert, doing her best to prevent her mother from getting upset. Instead of being a safe harbor where Kim could rest and be comforted, her mother was a turbulent ocean in which Kim had to work hard not to drown.

As an adult, Kim learned that her mother probably qualified for a diagnosis of borderline personality disorder. It has helped Kim to know that her mother was not well and that her own reactions to her mother were normal and understandable. It also helps her to step back from the words her mother said about her and realize that they are not true. The more she is able to set strong boundaries with her mother, the safer she feels to extend love and forgiveness.

While most mothers do not struggle with something as extreme as borderline personality disorder, we all occasionally say things we regret to our children. Likewise, we all sometimes lose control of our emotions. As mothers, we cannot be perfect in all we say and do. But we can and always should make repairs. If we can acknowledge and apologize for our blowups, we will restore our children to a state of feeling loved and safe.

Severe abuse by a mother is not familiar to most of us, but it is part of many women's stories and should not be ignored. Even though the following case may seem extreme, it is true. We have included it for those of you who did experience more serious abuse and for the lessons it might hold for the rest of us.

Christina Crawford, adopted daughter of Joan Crawford and author of the book *Mommie Dearest*, sat down with Larry King in 2001 to discuss the abuse she had survived as a child.[1] She admitted that her trouble began around age four or five when she started to become a person with her own likes and dislikes. Her mother would hit her for not picking up her clothes, for saying no, for a look, for an attitude, or for no obvious reason at all.

When Christina was thirteen, her mother knocked her to the floor and choked her. Christina believes her mother's intent was to kill her and that she might have succeeded if there had not been someone else in the house. She remembers her mother's eyes:

> She had gone into some other realm. She was like
> a wild animal. And at that age, to think that the
> person that you're supposed to love and trust the
> most is the person that just tried to kill you—that
> is almost too much for anybody to handle at that
> young age.[2]

When her mother's health declined, Christina became her caregiver, only to be surprised by the words in her mother's will: "I leave nothing to my daughter, Christina . . . for reasons that are well known to [her]."

> I tried very hard to love her because she was the
> only mother that I knew. . . . When she died, I was
> the only one to go and see her body (partly because
> I had to assure myself . . . that she was really dead.
> . . . I had to assure myself that she wasn't going to
> get up and start yelling at me again). . . . It was the
> best thing that I could have done. . . . I told her then
> that I loved her, which was true in the sense that I
> had tried to love her. I don't think that she ever was
> capable of loving me, but I think she tried.[3]

When Larry King asked Christina if her relationship with her mother led to difficulty in her own relationships,

Christina replied, "Always." At the time of the interview, Christina was sixty-two and not married; she said that "it was impossible to trust anybody." When asked why she never adopted a child, she replied, "Most of my life was so unstable, both emotionally and financially, that I couldn't in good conscience visit on somebody else what had been visited on me."[4]

Abuse is never a child's fault, but it often seems so in her mind. *If only I were better, then things would be different. Maybe if I . . . Mom would not be so mad at me, would not say mean things, or would be more loving.* When a mother is more concerned about herself than about her child, she often leaves her daughter with a poor self-concept and the inability to let others in.

2. Mom Doesn't Protect Us from Others

Some mothers may never strike their daughters or call them demeaning names. Yet if a mother stands by and doesn't act when she sees her daughter being physically, sexually, verbally, or emotionally abused, she is shirking one of her most important duties as a parent and her daughter will feel betrayed by her.

Margaret lived with her mother and a volatile stepfather. On most nights Margaret's stepfather would come home from work, eat dinner, and then sit silently in front of the television. Margaret and her mother walked on eggshells all night, fearing something would set him off.

"We never knew when he would blow or what would make it happen—a charred roast, a stain on the carpet, an innocent remark. Whatever the reason, it was as if a match were thrown into a pile of dynamite and he would explode. He yelled and cursed and called us names. He threw dishes and punched holes in the walls. Once he grabbed my mom by the hair and dragged her across the kitchen to clean up a mess. I used to beg my mom to take us to live somewhere else, but she wouldn't do it. I think she was afraid—afraid to make him even madder, afraid she couldn't live without him. She would make excuses for him such as 'He had a rough day' or 'I shouldn't have burned the dinner.' When it was really bad, she would despairingly say, 'Where else would we go?'"

Margaret is closely bonded to her mother because they endured the abusive episodes together—it was their private secret. However, she is also incensed with her mother for allowing the abuse to continue. Where was the "mama bear" that was supposed to protect her cub? Margaret concluded that her mother valued her husband more than her, which was painful to admit.

As an adult, Margaret has a hard time advocating for herself or standing up to others. She follows the pattern she learned from her mother. In order to survive in the world, especially with men, she toes the line and never does anything that might make someone angry.

Unfortunately, a mother can be afraid to rock the boat with her husband, fearing he would retaliate and withhold love from her. When he mistreats the children, she thinks it will blow over or that the children should adjust. But a child without an advocate is a child who is defenseless, unable to fight against a parent or stepparent's abuse.

Angry outbursts are not the only thing that affects a child. Abuse in any form is something that every daughter, every child needs to be protected from.

Adrienne lives with the reality of having been sexually abused by her own father. She was always a pretty little girl who received lots of attention for her looks. As she grew up, her father's affection for her increased. At first it was snuggling and hugs and sitting on his lap. Before long there were secrets she was told to keep: the way he taught her to touch him and the way he began touching her. Adrienne was confused and afraid, but he said if she mentioned anything to her mother, the family would fall apart. She believed him and kept quiet.

Then one morning, she decided to break the silence and talked to her mother, certain she would be protected. Her mother's response was unexpected. "I know. I've always known. But your daddy loves you, and besides, men will be men."

Shocked and sad, Adrienne began to stay away from home more and more. She eventually ran away and was taken in by her best friend's family. In the end, both of her parents hurt her. It was her father who abused her, but the mommy she thought lived to love and protect her did not keep her safe.

Judi wasn't sexually abused, but she was tormented by her older siblings, who often made fun of her slight speech impediment and called her a mama's girl. Her mother downplayed what Judi's siblings were doing and often laughed along at the things they were saying to her. "They are just poking fun, being little comedians."

To this day some of the things Judi's siblings said haunt her, pulling her into insecurity. She wasn't safe in her own family with her own siblings, so how could she be safe anywhere? Though she has a love-hate relationship with her siblings as an adult, Judi feels most betrayed by her mother. The woman who could have stopped the remarks and teasing didn't. Judi grew up feeling unsafe and unloved.

3. Mom Models Fearfulness

A fearful, overprotective mother can create fear in her child. When both the mother and the child are caught in this web of emotional fear, any semblance of safety is lost in the ongoing turmoil over small things that should easily be remedied.

Emma was an outgoing little girl with a full measure of energy, but her mother was fearful of most activities. Still, when Emma asked if she could take swimming lessons, her mother reluctantly agreed.

While the other children bobbed up and down, sometimes swallowing a mouthful of water, Emma stayed close to the side of the pool, where her mother called out nervous instructions.

When the swim teacher directed everyone to the diving board, Emma got in line and waved excitedly to her mom. As soon as Emma got to the edge of the board, her mom panicked. "No, no, no, she is too young. Come off the board, Emma!" Emma retraced her steps and let the other swimmers go ahead of her.

All the other kids jumped off the diving board and celebrated their victory—everyone except Emma. Her mother thought she was protecting Emma with her concern, but she actually was teaching Emma to be fearful. Over time the fears quenched Emma's energy and curiosity, and her personality changed from fun-loving to timid. Sadly, her mother's anxieties took root in Emma, and she became reluctant to try new things.

GOD IS TRUSTWORTHY

In many ways, our mothers mirror God, but because they are human they fall short. Although God doesn't promise to always keep us safe from harm in this world, he is completely trustworthy. Jesus gave his disciples this assurance:

I have told you these things, so that in me you may have peace. In this world you will have trouble. But take heart! I have overcome the world.

JOHN 16:33, NIV

Life will be hard, but God will be with us every moment until *ultimately* we are safe with him forever. Though our bodies may not always be safe, our souls are safe in him.

It is God's character to protect our hearts and souls no matter what we go through. The psalmist elaborated on this by describing God as our shield, our strong tower, our shepherd, our refuge, our keeper, our rock, our shade, and our hiding place (see Psalm 23; Psalm 32, NIV; Psalm 34; Psalm 91; Psalm 121, ESV; Psalm 144).

We are to trust in him with all our hearts and lean not on our own understanding (see Proverbs 3:5-6, NIV). This requires faith and provides hope. We need to embrace him for who he says he is, believing his promises—not what our wounds tell us.

Explore Your Story

1. What emotions do the stories in this chapter evoke in you? Can you relate to having a mother who was unsafe or did not look after your physical and emotional welfare? Was your mother able to regulate her own emotions?

2. Prayerfully journal the story of why you did or did not feel safe and what messages were pressed into your soul as a child. As you unravel your thoughts over time, God will reveal areas that need healing.

3. How do those imprinted messages continue to affect you today?

4. What truths about God's protection and trustworthiness resonate with you and why?

Connect with God

Lord, I may never fully understand why I went through some of the things I did, but I am grateful that you ultimately have kept me safe and are now healing my residual wounds. I come to you with my deep-seated fears. Please direct my heart, mind, and soul to a safe place today. Destroy the walls of fear and anxiety that have prevented me from living a courageous and secure life in you. Father, fulfill your promise and deliver me. Amen.

7

mom, will you teach and guide me?

Our children are watching us live,
and what we are shouts louder than anything we can say.

WILFRED PETERSON

CHILDREN COME INTO THIS WORLD without wisdom or skills to deal with the challenges of life. They need adults to shepherd them, instruct them, lead them, and be their example. Without that leadership and guidance, they often flounder, trying to do the best they can.

Verbal instruction and training are important, but the *example* a mother sets leaves the deepest impression on a daughter. More is caught than is taught. Scripture emphasizes the importance of exemplifying good character in the way we live:

Be their ideal; let them follow the way you teach and
live; be a pattern for them in your love, your faith,
and your clean thoughts.

I TIMOTHY 4:12, TLB

Every day, a mother's words and deeds are woven into her
little girl's heart and mind and ultimately shape what kind
of woman she becomes and how she fits into the fabric of
her world.

MOM, WILL YOU MOTHER ME?

Some mothers abdicate their leadership role. They leave their
daughters to figure things out on their own. Or they may
reverse roles, relying on their children to be in charge and
care for them. A child who is pushed into the role of parent
in the family is often called a "parentified child."

Collette described her mother as "wimpy." "My
mom was so shy she barely spoke to people. She had
no confidence and was often overwhelmed by the
smallest problems. Because she didn't teach me how to
deal with life, I was pretty much on my own to figure
things out. I developed a tough exterior and made it
look as if I could handle everything. But on the inside,
I was a little girl who wasn't sure she could cope. And
yet I would give my mom emotional support more
often than she would give it to me.

"When I was a teenager, she once asked me to help her make a doctor's appointment. I yelled at her, 'Why can't you grow up? You're supposed to be the mom, not me!' As I think back, I feel both sorry for her and sad for me. It was so frustrating to have her never even admit she had a problem, much less do anything about it.

"Even though I wish I could be close to people, I still have a hard time letting my walls down or letting people know I have needs. Some younger part of me still thinks it is dangerous to lean on others because if I ever tried to lean on my mom, I would always end up deeply disappointed."

While some mothers expect their children to "parent" them, other mothers try to create a peer relationship. Morgan's mother blurred the lines between parent and girlfriend.

Morgan's mother loved being the "cool, young mom." She enjoyed spending time with Morgan's high school friends and provided them with alcohol when they were in her home. She and Morgan shared clothing and did their hair in the same long, straight style. If one of Morgan's friends needed a parent to lie for them, she would do it. Morgan's mother joked provocatively with the boys Morgan brought home and complimented them on their muscles. She enjoyed knowing they found her attractive. She allowed Morgan's boyfriend to spend the night in Morgan's room.

Morgan was torn. She both liked and hated having the "cool mom." When she went to the homes of friends who had more mature parents, she envied the structure and limits her friends were given. It was scary to be given so much freedom at this age. She wished her mother would act more like a parent, would teach her what was right and wrong, and would sometimes say no to her.

Daughters who don't have a strong, guiding parental hand must find ways to cope. They may develop a tough exterior and become excessively self-reliant and independent. Or they may become excessively dependent, lacking a sense of self and looking to others for approval, direction, and identity. Both of these reactions to this momplication are likely to adversely affect future relationships if they are not addressed.

Do you relate to either of the women in these examples? I (Joan) know I can. If you were brought up by a parent who sometimes did not act like a parent, what do you wish your mother had done differently? If you are a mom, how do you want to parent your own children differently?

Teach Me Basic Life Skills

Did you feel prepared to face the world as an adult?

Rachel's father was in the navy and often would be at sea for months at a time. While he was away, Rachel's mother would go out and get drunk, not coming home until the middle of the night. Rachel and her sister were left to fend for themselves and eat whatever they could find—usually cold cereal. Rachel remembers the terror, the loneliness, and the longing for her mother.

Now a mother herself, Rachel struggles to prepare meals for herself and her family. She says, "It's as if there is a little girl inside me, waiting for her mommy to come and feed her."

Daughters like Rachel who were not taught life skills may have a harder time with day-to-day life. Whether it be doing a school project, applying to colleges, or developing a budget, they often must find other people or resources to help them. If they don't find help, they may lack confidence or avoid situations in which they don't feel capable. They may struggle in school or work because they have not been given habits of self-management and self-care.

Boost My Emotional Intelligence

Are you comfortable expressing your feelings and acknowledging your emotions? Or do your feelings overtake you, causing you to act in ways you later regret?

Cheri's mother was stoic and proud and thought emotional people were weak. When Cheri's pet rabbit died, her mother told her to "buck up and be strong." Cheri was devastated, but because she wasn't taught how to navigate sadness, she found other ways to feel better. One of her primary coping methods was to eat as a way to numb her feelings.

In contrast, Kathi's mother vented her emotions freely and

without self-control, taking her family on a roller coaster of ups and downs. She would yell if she was frustrated or sob loudly behind a locked bedroom door if she was unhappy. This out-of-control environment was scary to Kathi and her sister, and each of them coped differently. Kathi's sister responded by trying to care for and manage her mother. She would walk on eggshells and put her own feelings aside in an attempt to keep her mother calm. Kathi, on the other hand, became a lot like her mother. In her teen years, she and her mother would have screaming, hitting battles. Kathi has had to work hard to develop the skill of keeping her emotions in check.

We all know about the intelligence quotient (IQ), but what about emotional intelligence (EQ)? According to Daniel Goleman, author of the book *Emotional Intelligence*,[1] EQ is a far higher predictor of success in life than IQ. The ability to manage one's emotions and to empathize with the emotions of others is a crucial skill for children to learn. Ideally, a mother will see and validate her child's emotions and help the child name them. She might say, "I see you are feeling mad" or "Do you have that sad, lonely feeling right now?" By doing this, she helps her child avoid both extremes; she teaches her to neither deny her emotions nor be overwhelmed by them.

Define Womanhood for Me

What does it mean to you to be a woman? While the answer to that question will vary from culture to culture, daughters look to their mothers to define womanhood for them.

Children look to both parents for love and guidance, but they gravitate to one parent for more gender-specific knowledge. Boys look to their fathers to learn what it means to be a man, while girls look to their mothers to learn what it means to be a woman. Just the other day my (Debbie's) own four-year-old granddaughter Jessa announced to me with great conviction and joy, "Grammy, you are a woman, and I am a little woman!" I had to laugh, but I quickly realized that this little girl is already identifying in specific ways with the females in her life.

In her book *Motherless Daughters*, Hope Edelman discusses a repeated lament she has heard from women who lost their mothers at a young age. Hard as a single father may try, he cannot always teach his daughter the feminine ins and outs of navigating the world. These women complained that they didn't know how to do certain female-oriented things, such as choosing a dress for a school dance or finding an appropriate gift for a wedding shower. They believed they hadn't learned "the code" and felt a huge hole in their understanding of a woman's world.[2]

Help Me Love My Body

What did you grow up thinking about your body? What did your mother model for you? What guidance did she give you?

Karen grew up with a mother who did not take care of herself physically. She was always at least a hundred pounds overweight but laughed about her size as if it were nothing. When Karen became a teen, she was embarrassed by the fattening foods her mother always ordered and how sloppy she was at the table. Karen knew her mother's weight affected her mom's relationships and health. She vowed to never allow herself to go down that path. As a result, Karen grew up controlling her weight by purging with laxatives and exercising compulsively. She did not admit to having an eating disorder, but it was obvious to everyone else.

Laurie's mother was beautiful but obsessed with staying young. When she noticed faint lines on her forehead, a little roll around her middle, and a few gray hairs, she was horrified. The message Laurie received was that aging was terrible. Not surprisingly, Laurie became consumed with her appearance. Like her mother, Laurie would not leave the house unless she was in full makeup and dressed to the nines. Sadly, Laurie carried this mind-set into her marriage and growing family. After some time with a skilled counselor, Laurie began to see that her mother had modeled bondage, not freedom. What her mother thought was the way to youth and beauty was actually a trap of self-focus and insecurity.

In both of these scenarios, the mother did not teach her daughter how to accept and appreciate her own body. Mothers have a huge influence on their daughters' body perception and beliefs about their appearance. Often a mother doesn't realize how much her example and her view of herself are rubbing off on her daughter. There are two ways this can get skewed. On one hand, training a daughter to be responsible about self-care is important, but on the other hand, it can become an obsession. If a mom has a healthy view of herself, then the daughter will likely grow up with a healthy self-perception as well. But if the mother never misses a workout, never stops counting calories, and constantly demeans herself and her body, her daughter will be affected. Our mothers convey whether our bodies are something to be celebrated or something to be ashamed of.

Show Me How to Relate to Men

What example did your mother set for you regarding men? Did you see her dominating them or hear her speaking about them with contempt? Did she submerge herself in her man, never speaking up for herself or setting boundaries? Did she convey the belief that men were not to be trusted, that you had to do everything on your own? Did she manipulate or flirt with men to get what she wanted? What messages did you internalize, maybe without even realizing it? Perhaps you are like your mother, or perhaps you vowed to be different.

Marissa thought her mother acted like a doormat, allowing her husband to walk all over her. She never stood up for herself or expressed her own thoughts or opinions. Marissa's father was a Democrat, so her mother was a Democrat. If her father wanted to spend the afternoon watching football, her mother spent the afternoon watching football. Whenever Marissa's father was in a foul mood, her mother would scramble to appease him, even if it meant putting her needs and the children's needs aside.

Marissa vowed she would never allow a man to treat her the way her father had treated her mother. Rather than entering relationships with an open heart, she came with her fists up, ready to fight any hint of domination by a man. When she was thirty-three, she went to therapy to understand why she couldn't maintain a good romantic relationship. As she explored what had been modeled for her and how she had overreacted to it, she began to see that part of her feared that if she let a man in, she would become like her mother.

In contrast, Serene's parents had a strained relationship, and all she heard was her mother's negative comments about men. Serene grew up believing all men were selfish, stupid, and only interested in sex. Serene was not equipped to love a man for who he was. Her attitude toward men cost her two marriages where she punished her husbands by withholding sex, and a few jobs where she could not get along with male superiors.

Introduce Me to God

What did you learn about God from observing your mother?

The most important thing a mother can model for her daughter is a close relationship with God. I (Joan) learned from my mother that there was no God, and eventually I took on the worldview that I could only depend on myself. So when tragedy struck, I was not connected to a heavenly parent who could ultimately make sense of things and offer me comfort, hope, and healing.

Other mothers may convey different wrong beliefs about God through their words or actions. They may send the message that he is harsh, indifferent, or unloving.

Carla was raised by a devout mother who took her to church each week but rarely talked to her about God. She left

Carla's spiritual training to the "professionals" at church. Carla was taught more about church practices than about having a personal relationship with God. She was under the impression that you could only call upon God in a crisis. Carla left the church after high school and never looked back—she had no interest in God at all. When she became a mother, she felt lost and unable to guide her children on a spiritual path.

Leslie grew up in a strict religious home. Her childhood memories are filled with church meetings and countless rules. Life was serious and hard, not filled with joy and laughter. Her mother did not celebrate birthdays or holidays.

As an adult, Leslie shunned anything that remotely smacked of God-talk until she had children of her own. She began longing to know God in a different way. Her life was changed forever when she met the God of love and grace at an old-fashioned revival meeting.

Why does teaching our daughters about God matter? Because it matters to him. God instructs parents to train their children about spiritual matters, inviting his presence into their family.

Train up a child in the way she should go,
Even when she is old she will not depart from it.
ADAPTED FROM PROVERBS 22:6, NASB

Love the LORD your God with all your heart and
with all your soul and with all your strength. These
commandments that I give you today are to be on your

hearts. Impress them on your children. Talk about
them when you sit at home and when you walk along
the road, when you lie down and when you get up.

DEUTERONOMY 6:5-7, NIV

GOD'S PROMISE

Whether or not our mothers were strong leaders and gave
us the guidance we needed to prepare us for life, we all need
God to show us the way more clearly. Listening to God and
following him is the most important thing for us to learn.

I will instruct you and teach you in the way you
should go;
I will counsel you with my loving eye on you.

PSALM 32:8, NIV

The teaching of your word gives light,
so even the simple can understand. . . .
Guide my steps by your word,
so I will not be overcome by evil. . . .
Look upon me with love;
teach me your decrees.

PSALM 119:130, 133, 135

Your hands made me and formed me;
give me understanding to learn your commands.

PSALM 119:73, NIV

In addition to Scripture, God also provides another way to guide us onto the right path: the presence of the Holy Spirit. Jesus taught his disciples many things in the three years they were together. Anticipating his return to his Father after his death and resurrection, Jesus assured the disciples they would not be left alone. He would not be with them physically, but in his place, God would provide the perfect Counselor.

> I will ask the Father, and he will give you another advocate to help you and be with you forever—the Spirit of truth. . . . He lives with you and will be in you. I will not leave you as orphans; I will come to you. . . . But the Advocate, the Holy Spirit, whom the Father will send in my name, will teach you all things and will remind you of everything I have said to you. Peace I leave with you.
>
> JOHN 14:16-18, 26-27, NIV

Do you see yourself in this chapter? If you are a mom, are you afraid that you have messed up your children by not teaching them the right things? Take heart. Remember that God is the author of every story. He is leading and guiding us. And he offers redemption and new direction for our children. Despite our parenting mistakes, we can trust that nothing is beyond God's healing. As our daughters grow up to make their own choices, God will always be with them to lead them and guide them, too.

Explore Your Story

1. What emotions do the stories in this chapter evoke in you? Did they point to areas in your life where you do not feel you received the leadership, guidance, or teaching you needed?

2. Prayerfully journal about the ways your mother did or did not lead, teach, or set a positive example for you.

3. How do the things you journaled about in question 2 continue to affect you today?

4. What truths about God's instruction and guidance speak to you and why?

Connect with God

Lord, thank you for being my Shepherd who promises to instruct me and teach me in the way that I should go. I come to you for more training. My mother did what she could to help me understand who I am and how my life fits into this world, but there are still holes left in my education that need to be filled. Lead each of my steps. Guide me through each assignment, each responsibility, and each relationship I form from this day forward. Be my trainer, coach, and counselor. Amen.

8

mom, will you celebrate me as a unique individual?

You is kind. You is smart. You is important.

FROM *The Help*

"JOANIE! Mommy's home!"

I jumped up and ran to the small entryway of our house. Annie toddled up next to me.

My mother wasn't in her usual blue jeans. Instead, she wore a skirt, high heels, and nylon stockings. Her dark hair was short, and her lipstick was bright red. She reminded me of Elizabeth Taylor, whose picture I had seen on the cover of *Life* magazine.

"Mommy, you look pretty."

Her eyes sparkled and her smile was huge.

"Thank you, Joanie."

Placing her purse on the table, she responded to Annie's

upstretched arms. After nuzzling Annie's neck with kisses, she turned her gaze on me. It was as if she were appraising me, examining me, looking for something she hadn't seen before.

The babysitter's voice came from down the hall. "I'm changing Johnny's diaper. I'll be there in a minute."

"Okay," my mom called back as she put Annie down and reached over to give me a hug and a kiss on the cheek.

"Come here for a minute, Joanie," she said as she stepped into the living room and sat on the couch.

I stood facing her as she continued to study me.

"I was just at a meeting with your teacher. Mrs. Lang said you are very smart. She said you scored above most other kids in the country on that test you took. She showed it to me, and we were both surprised at what you knew. How did you know what a dome was?" She looked at me curiously, as if I were a marvelous, mysterious thing.

"I don't know. I just knew," I replied, shrugging my shoulders.

"Well, she said you are very smart."

My mother's delight felt like warm honey pouring over me. When she was happy, I felt happy. But this was even better because she was happy with *me*. *I made Mommy's eyes sparkle, and she's smiling. There must be something very good about me.*

Both mothers and fathers have a profound ability to build up a daughter's sense of self through affirming words and actions. Their words are often pressed into the child's soul and become part of her default network. Mothers are particularly powerful in the early life of a girl because the child has minimal capacity to know herself as separate from her mother. Another important aspect of a girl's experience growing up is finding out who she is apart from her mother. Difficult as it sometimes is, mothers need to embrace how their daughters are different and be their cheerleaders as they go on separate paths.

To summarize, there are two ways daughters need to be celebrated by their mothers:

> *A daughter needs to receive positive messages about her value and who she is.*
> *A daughter needs to be encouraged to find her own distinct identity.*

If a mother does not affirm her daughter or if she does not encourage her to find her own separate identity, the daughter may begin to form distorted beliefs about herself. She may not realize that she is a precious, unique woman who can have her own personality, talents, dreams, interests, relationships, and life work. *Individuation* is the term used in psychology to describe the natural separation from family that a child must undergo. It is the ability to be oneself, while staying connected to the others in the family.

What does a daughter with a strong sense of self look like? She is someone who

- *Has self-respect and self-worth*
- *Has a deep core sense of "I am okay" and "I am enough"*
- *Can look within and name her own likes and dislikes, her own opinions and values*
- *Can name, honor, and regulate her own emotions*
- *Can choose her own life path, despite opposition from others*
- *Can maintain strong personal boundaries*
- *Can speak up and defend herself against mistreatment*
- *Can face and admit her own wrongdoings*
- *Is willing to try new things and embrace failures as opportunities to grow*
- *Is willing to end unhealthy relationships*
- *Believes she can succeed at most things she sets out to do*
- *Has positive inner self-talk—"I'm strong. I can do this."*
- *Has courage and confidence*
- *Appreciates and accepts her body as it is*
- *Believes her value as a female is equal to that of males*
- *Believes her value goes beyond her body or her sexuality*
- *Has no need to be the "good girl" or "pleaser" or "superstar"*
- *Does not need to be better than others to feel good about herself*
- *Can tend to her own needs and ask for what she needs; has good self-care*

These women are likely to succeed in whatever they decide to do. Whether they are stay-at-home moms or CEOs, they live life with self-assurance and motivation. Those who have decided to become Christ followers aim to demonstrate godly love to others. They invite the Holy Spirit to be their inner guide. As they mature in their Christian life, they are less focused on their own desires, because they are consumed with the joy of knowing they belong to God. They see all that they have and all that they are as part of his ultimate story. In other words, they are validated in him.

> *Everything* got started in him and finds its purpose in him.
>
> COLOSSIANS 1:16-17, MSG

THE POWER OF A MOTHER'S WORDS

We've learned that from the moment a child is born, her mother's nonverbal cues speak volumes—in positive or negative ways. As the child grows and begins to understand what words mean, what her mother says has even more effect on her perception of her self-worth. As you know, these momplications can vary in severity. Maybe for you, your mother's words manifest like annoying mosquito bites, while for others, they can be deeply painful lacerations.

> Paula is a successful career woman, and she knows her mother loves her. They see each other weekly, and for the most part, Paula enjoys their time together. However, she does not enjoy her mother's

habit of "being helpful" by continually telling her how she could do better.

"That color is not the most flattering on you, dear."

"It would have been faster if you had turned at the last corner."

"You shouldn't have bought this couch. It looks shoddy."

While this barrage of little stings has not impaired Paula's ability to have an overall positive self-image or choose her own life path, it has implanted nagging questions in the back of Paula's mind: "Is my work good enough? Am I good enough?"

Ever since she was a little girl, she has tried hard to do things perfectly so her mother wouldn't criticize her. That desire to be perfect continues into her adult life. She wants her work, her appearance, and her house to be completely put together. This perfectionism causes anxiety and sometimes prevents her from taking risks. She struggles with procrastination when faced with important projects at work.

Paula needs to address these constant little "bites" from her mother in order for healing to begin. Not only do they impact Paula's life today, but they could affect the next generation in Paula's family. It will be difficult for Paula to resist the temptation to "perfect" her own children and correct them just as her mother constantly corrects her. Like Paula, her children may fear not living up to their mother's expectations.

Though overall Paula feels valued by her mother, many women do not feel that at all. The words spoken by some mothers qualify as verbal abuse, deeply wounding their daughters' sense of self.

Anita's mother is more than slightly critical. She is outright mean. Whatever pops into her head pops out of her mouth.

"You're fat."

"What's wrong with you?"

"How could you be such a fool?"

Anita knows that her mother was treated the same way by her grandmother, but that does not take away the hurt. Her mother's words have carved the message into her soul that she is inferior. Anita dreams of finishing college and teaching grade school, but she believes she doesn't have what it takes to accomplish that goal. She also longs for a happy marriage but repeatedly gets into relationships with selfish, mean men. In her mind, she believes that she does not deserve anything better.

What words do you remember your mother saying to you? Was her tone negative or positive? Do you find yourself still trying to please her? How have her words affected you?

Shame may be the foundation of who you are right now, but it doesn't have to stay that way. Once you have identified the beliefs about yourself that might be fueling performance anxiety, perfectionism, narcissism, or people pleasing, you can begin to rewrite them.

Does Your Mother Want You to Fit Her Mold?

All mothers have hopes and dreams for their daughters, but when a mother cannot put aside her own ideas of who her daughter should be, the results can be destructive.

> Peg's mother was ashamed to be the daughter of uneducated oil-refinery workers. She worked hard to be something different, and she succeeded when she married a doctor. She carefully cultivated her new identity as a well-read, impeccably dressed, country club socialite.
>
> When Peg and her sister were born, their mother wanted them to fit the picture—to be "little ladies" in appearance and behavior. Peg's older sister stepped right into line. Her long, straight blonde hair and big blue eyes made her look like a flawless china doll, and she was quiet and well-mannered. Peg, on the other hand, was unruly from the moment she came screaming out of her mother's womb. Her wiry, curly hair refused to be tamed, and she was loud, expressive, and messy.

For as long as Peg can remember, she just felt "wrong." Everyone else in her family toed the line for her mother. The almost constant disapproval from her mother, and later her sister, made her feel sad and lonely. Even when she became an adult, she knew that in her mother's view she had married the "wrong" man and chosen the "wrong" job. Neither provided the money or the status her mother regarded so highly. It hurt Peg to know that her mother was proud of her sister but not of her.

Peg's mother had not resolved the shame from her own childhood. There were still younger parts of her—parts that felt unacceptable in society—so she hid them away and could not tolerate any actions by her children that made those feelings return. She needed her children to maintain the facade. She needed them to be her reflection—to make her look good.

Though it might not seem like it, Peg's sister was wounded too. She embraced her mother's mold at the expense of her true self.

Is Your Mother Competitive or Narcissistic?

A mother who competes with her daughter is often a narcissist who needs the spotlight. When her position as top dog in the family is threatened, she panics. This mother inwardly struggles when a daughter defies her or is prettier or more accomplished than she is. She often is jealous when she sees her husband dote on their daughter rather than paying attention to her.

Daughters of these mothers come to believe they must remain small in order to be loved. If they rise up and do anything that threatens their mothers' place on center stage, they will become their mothers' enemies. A daughter's need for her mother's love and approval is so profound that she cannot allow that to happen, so she keeps her mother happy by becoming nearly invisible.

Chloe was excited to try on wedding dresses. Each time she came out of the dressing room to model a gown for her friends and family, everyone oohed and aahed—everyone except her mother. Once the commotion died down, Chloe turned to her mother, silently begging for her approval. Her mother, with a sucking-on-a-lemon look on her face, said, "Absolutely not." The bride-to-be tried on more gowns. "It looks cheap." "You don't have the figure for that dress." Her mother didn't even pretend to like any of the dresses. Chloe had hoped that wedding dress shopping would be a bonding experience for her and her mother. But instead it was a heartbreaking reminder that her mother always needed to redirect the attention to herself, hurting her daughter in the process.

Almost all of us occasionally display narcissistic traits, but some people have entrenched patterns of self-absorbed behavior. Narcissists are defined by these desires and actions:

- *They crave attention.*
- *They desperately need to feel superior to others.*
- *They are often competitive, manipulative, and demanding.*
- *They feel entitled to use or take advantage of others in order to achieve their own ends.*
- *They are self-absorbed and lack the ability to recognize or empathize with the needs and feelings of others.*
- *They may lie to make themselves look better or to ensure they come out on top in a conflict.*

A narcissistic mom has difficulty seeing her daughter as a separate human being. In the mother's view, she and her daughter are one and the same. Some mothers think this deep connection is a positive thing. As one mom said, "We love hanging out together. We wear each other's clothes and go to the same hairstylist. We are pretty much the same person." In reality, the daughter is trapped, unable to discover who she actually is. The psychological term for this is *enmeshment*. Enmeshment is a lack of healthy boundaries between mother and daughter. The mother's thoughts and feelings become the daughter's thoughts and feelings. The mother's opinions become the daughter's opinions. This mother often tries to live out her unrealized dreams through her daughter. The daughter's accomplishments are viewed by the mother as her own accomplishments. The daughter is not allowed to fail because the mother experiences it as her own failure.

If you have a narcissistic mother, she may have ruined

many special occasions and events. She may have gone as far as competing for your boyfriends or turning your own children against you. She may expect you to put your whole life aside so you can meet her needs. If you are one of these daughters, you need reparenting by God. You are important in God's eyes and have the right to follow the guidance of the Holy Spirit, not the twisted reasoning or lies of your mother.

Is Your Mother Controlling?

Some mothers override their daughters' sense of self by insisting that things be done their way. That was true for Lisa:

> I will never forget the day my mother cut my long hair. It wasn't my decision, but she didn't have the patience to listen to me crying over tangled hair. So, in early grade school it was cut off. From that point on, my mother refused to let me grow my hair out. I was in high school in the seventies when all the other girls had long hair parted down the middle. As I look back, I can now see that I slowly lost a sense of self, not knowing what I liked or didn't like, what my style was, etc. I looked to my mother to approve of things. Later I looked to my peers and became a people pleaser. I didn't realize it was okay to be me and to have my own likes and dislikes.

If you are a daughter of a controlling mother, you may have developed a facade of who you think you are supposed to be, while your true self is deeply buried.

Sheila was raised by a controlling Christian mother. She was not allowed to question the beliefs her mother held so firmly. Consequently, she did not develop her own faith or her own sense of values. To survive in her family, she became two different Sheilas. At home she was compliant and obedient. To avoid punishment, she spent her time at church, youth groups, and camps. But when she was out from under her mother's control, Sheila drank and was sexually active. Her church friends thought she was a spiritual leader, and her partying friends thought she was a wild girl.

If your mother was controlling, there's a good chance you lack your own values and goals. You may need to explore who you are, as opposed to who your mother told you to be.

Did Your Mother Too Readily Rescue You?

In the previous stories the mothers squelched their daughters' identities by being overbearing and wanting their daughters to exist to meet their desires. However, mothers can err at the opposite extreme when they do not impose strong limits or require enough from their daughters. These moms seem to be kind and generous, but they impede their daughters' development by not allowing them to struggle, learn from their mistakes, and develop responsibility. They may also teach their children that they deserve to be served and do not need to serve others.

You have probably heard the term "helicopter mom." Helicopter moms tend to be ordinary, well-meaning parents who love their children but take their parenting too far. They overparent, overprotect, and overperfect. They may be compensating for a deficit in the way they were parented, they may be acting out of their own fears, or they may be responding to pressure from others. Whatever the reason, the results are harmful to the child. By not standing back and encouraging their children to do things they are mentally and physically ready to do—by not letting them dig deep, struggle, and develop their own inner resources—helicopter moms rob their children of the ability to stand on their own two feet and be effective, self-motivated adults.

When Candace was born, her mother vowed she would be the "best mom ever." She determined that her daughter would never feel the abandonment or the loneliness she had experienced as a child. Candace's mom quit her job, read every parenting book she could find, hung a brain-stimulating mobile over Candace's crib, and made organic baby food.

"All that attention was probably great when I was a baby," said Candace, "yet as an adult I realize that my mom, despite all her good intentions, kind of crippled me. She did everything for me and barely required anything from me. I never had to do chores. I never learned to budget money. When the demands of the swim team got difficult for me, I quit. If my homework was too hard, Mom did it for me. If I had trouble with friends, she would call their parents. She didn't make me face the consequences of my decisions. She could not tolerate my feeling any pain.

"There is still a part of me that thinks life should be easy and that I should always be doted on. I started therapy because I was having a hard time finding and holding a good job. I wanted to *be* something great, but I did not want to go through the pain and hard work it takes to make something great happen. I kept waiting for God or someone else to make it easy for me, just as my mother had always done.

"I'm learning perseverance. I know that I am not entitled to any more luxury or comfort or privilege than anyone else. Yet that younger part of me that was coddled by Mom keeps jumping up and getting in my way. I am working hard to behave out of my adult self rather than out of those habits that were impressed on me when I was young."

Candace was disabled by her mother's hovering over-attention. Her mother provided her with a secure base, but she didn't step back so Candace could develop her own capabilities. She didn't train her to go into the world on her own with strength and independence.

There needs to be a balance, where moms neither squelch their children's individuality nor coddle or require too little of them. Amy Chua, in her book *Battle Hymn of the Tiger Mother*, said she was grateful for her strict upbringing, and she is raising her own children the same way. She related the story of making her child sit at the piano until she learned to play a piece, without dinner or water and under threat of losing her dollhouse.[1] She maintained that Americans tend to be too indulgent with their children and that Chinese children have more academic success because they are treated strictly.[2] Others argue with her that excessive pressure to succeed can lead to anxiety and, in extreme cases, even suicide in young students. This is a debate not only between parents but between cultures. In general, Americans tend to more highly value individual expression, while many other cultures tend to give family and community a higher priority. What has your culture taught you about this issue?

A word of caution: Affirmation or rewards that are given too easily do not motivate. Children sense when rewards are empty and not deserved. A "Good job" or "You have a gift" from a tough coach carries far more weight than affirmation that is frequently given to everyone. If there has been minimal challenge or if all who play get a trophy, the trophy doesn't mean much. Children who receive easy rewards become entitled. They are robbed of the satisfaction of pulling deep from within themselves to overcome challenges.

A parent's goal is to find the sweet spot where a child knows she is loved unconditionally but also knows that how she performs will directly relate to consequences in her life.

GOD CELEBRATES YOU

Do you believe that you were created by God for a purpose? Do you know he esteems you, values you, and celebrates you? Do you grasp that you are his masterpiece, unlike anyone else, with gifts and callings that are uniquely yours?

Stop for a moment and let this truth sink in:

You are a holy people, who belong to the LORD your God. Of all the people on earth, the LORD your God has chosen you to be his own special treasure.

DEUTERONOMY 7:6

Say it to yourself: "He has chosen me. I am his own special treasure."

Some of the descriptions of mothers in this chapter may have struck a chord with you, and some may not. There are probably ways your mother has called out the best in you and ways she has not. No matter what, you are not defined by your mother or your past or even by yourself. You are defined by God. He knows you best—inside and out. C. S. Lewis has reminded us of the most basic truth about our identity: "This is the marvel of marvels, that he called me Beloved."[3]

Explore Your Story

1. What emotions do the stories in this chapter evoke in you? Did your mother celebrate your value? Were most of her words kind and encouraging, or did they tend to be critical and mean?

2. Did your mother encourage you to find your own identity and your own path, or did she have trouble letting you be a separate individual? Was she similar to any of the profiles in this chapter: narcissistic, competitive, controlling, overinvolved, or a "helicopter mom"?

3. Did your mother tend to be strict or permissive? Did she require responsibility from you or coddle you? Did she challenge you to do your best or too readily give you undeserved praise and rewards?

4. How do the beliefs about yourself that you received from your mother continue to affect you today? Are they deep knife cuts or minor mosquito bites? As you read through the traits of someone with a strong sense of self, how many of them describe you?

5. As you read about God's celebration of who you are, what truths speak to your heart?

Connect with God

Lord, thank you that in Christ I am your beloved daughter whom you love, with whom you are well pleased. Help me to see myself through your eyes. Shine your light on my distorted beliefs and unhealthy patterns so they can be replaced by your truth. Free me to be the masterpiece you created me to be, and equip me to do the good works you planned for me to do. Thank you for your song of victory and celebration over my life. May your song become the song of my soul, the joy for my path, and the healing for my heart. Amen.

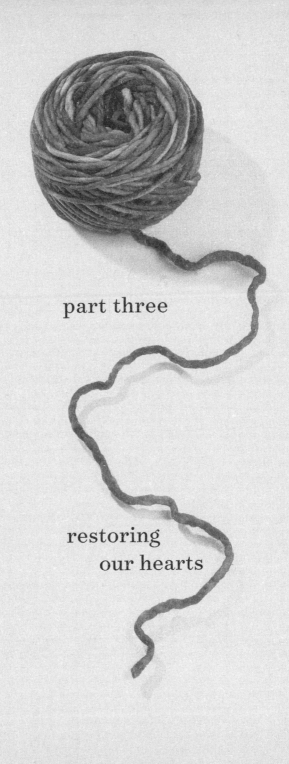

part three

restoring
our hearts

God took hold of you to restore to you what the enemy had stolen from you, but you will need to be determined to have it back. Do not be passive and expect victory to just fall on you. It does come by the grace of God, and not by our works, but we must actively cooperate with the Holy Spirit each step of the way.

JOYCE MEYER, *Beauty for Ashes*

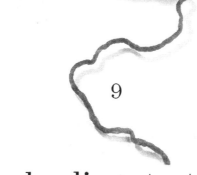

9

healing starts
with facing reality

Growth will never happen in our lives until
we value facing truth more than avoiding pain.

JOHN ORTBERG

THE MOTHER-DAUGHTER RELATIONSHIP IS certainly momplicated, isn't it? Did any of the four needs discussed in chapters
5 through 8 resonate with you? You may have been surprised
to see ways in which your mother did not perfectly meet your
needs. Now that you have identified these areas, you can
begin to pursue healing. Not only does healing relieve our
pain, but it also helps us become the women of love, truth,
and integrity that God designed us to be. Are you ready to
embrace the life that Jesus offers?

WHAT DOES HEALING LOOK LIKE?

There are two levels of healing with our mothers: One is external, and one is internal. While we may long for external healing—to resolve our conflicts, to have our mothers show us love, to be close to them and nurtured by them—reality determines whether or not this is possible. Much depends on whether your mother is still living and whether she is willing to do her part to heal the relationship. (We will talk about that aspect of healing in chapter 11.)

On the other hand, internal healing is something you do on your own, and it is always possible. The first step to repairing any relationship is to stop pointing fingers at the other person and focus on ourselves. You are the only person you ultimately have the power to change.

The goal is to live out of our true adult selves, rather than out of our childhood wounds or patterns. For Christians, this adult life is characterized by the fruit of the Holy Spirit: love, joy, peace, patience, kindness, goodness, faithfulness, gentleness, and self-control (see Galatians 5:22-23). It is a life of less unnecessary pain and more purpose. It is a life that God can use to significantly impact our families and our worlds.

Neither of us dived deeply into our mother-daughter healing journeys until after our mothers had passed away. I (Debbie) sought counseling in my fifties and was surprised to learn that a current situation was triggering feelings of rejection that had developed in my early relationship with my mother. I (Joan) always knew I had "daddy issues," but as I worked on this book, I discovered how many of my struggles are actually "mommy issues."

Healing is a process—we won't reach perfection in this life—and we are both still very much in the middle of the process! The apostle Paul described it well: "I don't mean to say that I have already achieved these things or that I have already reached perfection. But I press on to possess that perfection for which Christ Jesus first possessed me" (Philippians 3:12).

THE STEPS TO HEALING

There's no real formula for healing—it is supernatural, the work of the Holy Spirit. But if you don't know where to begin, we offer six steps to healing throughout the next two chapters. These will give you a path to follow. As we look back over our personal journeys and the women we have worked with, these steps are some of the touchstones we observed along the way. Keep in mind that the work of God cannot be reduced to a simple step-by-step process. Steps are merely tools to help us connect with God as we move toward healing. Also, remember that God is the ultimate healer, and healing comes in his time.

Step 1: Pray

We can read books, process our pain, and invest hours talking to a therapist, life coach, pastor, or friend, but in the end, help and healing come from the Spirit of the living God. He moves in the deepest places of our hearts—places we cannot get to on our own. Our first step toward unraveling our momplications is to pray.

In *The Circle Maker*, Mark Batterson encouraged big prayers and bold faith: "Don't just read the Bible. Start circling the promises. Don't just make a wish. Write down a list of God-glorifying life goals. Don't just pray. Keep a prayer journal."[1] The posture of prayer becomes practical as we begin to stand on the truth of God's promises.

In a later book, Batterson reiterated how powerful prayer is:

> I believe that every breakthrough, every blessing,
> every miracle, and every dream has a genealogy. If
> you trace it all the way back, you will find a prayer.
> Miracles are the product of prayers that were prayed
> by you or for you.[2]

Are you ready to tap into this powerful one-on-one conversation with God? Beginning each day in prayer lays a foundation of hope for the upcoming day. We connect with God, and we proclaim the hope that he is leading us in each day, through every part of our story, including the process of inner healing.

Ask God for his Kingdom to come and his will to be done as you embark on this healing journey. What would it look like for our lives to be directed by God's Kingdom, rather than our childhood programming? According to 2 Corinthians 3:17, it would be freedom, for "wherever the Spirit of the

Lord is, there is freedom." Prayer invites the Spirit of God to rule, so our past messages no longer run our lives.

Understandably, some women may feel blocked in their prayers because of the old lies that hold them back; it can be easy to believe that God doesn't care or that he won't hear or answer them. Yet Scripture tells a different story:

> We do not have a high priest who is unable to empathize with our weaknesses, but we have one who has been tempted in every way, just as we are—yet he did not sin. Let us then approach God's throne of grace with confidence, so that we may receive mercy and find grace to help us in our time of need.
>
> HEBREWS 4:15-16, NIV

Hold on to the key truths hidden in this passage to combat your doubts:

- *You have a God who understands you.*
- *You are to approach him confidently in prayer, knowing he loves you unconditionally.*
- *God cares about your pain, misbeliefs, and weaknesses.*
- *God has walked through life in human form, so he empathizes with your struggles and has much to teach you.*
- *You are invited to come to him to receive mercy and grace.*

Through prayer, we ask God to heal the wounds and rewrite the lies we have received from our mother-daughter relationships. He may answer this prayer immediately, but more often he leads us on a journey of renewal that may last a lifetime. Talk to him. Ask him to heal your pain, bind up your broken heart, bring you freedom, and help you grow. Invite him to use whatever means he desires to change your deepest imprints. Let him lead you and show you what specific steps toward healing he wants you to take. Trust him to use your wounds as openings through which his Spirit can enter and give you joy and peace.

God has answered our prayers to heal our mother wounds in miraculous ways, and we want that to happen for you, too. He will answer in his own way and in his own time. But no matter what, we agree with this conclusion:

> *He answers every prayer, and He keeps every promise.* That is who He is. That is what He does. And if you have the faith to dream big, pray hard, and think long, there is nothing God loves more than proving His faithfulness.[3]

Step 2: Identify Core Lies

It has been theorized that each of us holds three to five core lies about ourselves or God. These false beliefs were usually engraved in our souls early in our lives, when our hearts and minds were soft and receptive. Unchallenged, these lies can hold us in hurtful and negative patterns. For me (Debbie), one of my primary lies was "There is something wrong with me." In my young mind, it was the only way I could explain why my mother was cold and rejected me throughout my childhood. For me (Joan), a lie I believed was "I have no one to rely on but myself." That was my conclusion after my father died and my mother emotionally checked out.

What are the core lies that are shadows in your heart? Again, this is not about blaming our mothers but about identifying the negative beliefs that keep us stuck in pain or dysfunction and replacing those lies with truth. Do you struggle with any of the following false beliefs?

- *I am alone.*
- *I can only rely on myself.*
- *I do not belong.*
- *I can't do things well enough.*
- *I don't measure up.*
- *I must always protect myself.*
- *It is never safe to trust others.*
- *I don't have what it takes.*
- *I am always wrong.*
- *It's always my fault.*
- *I'm responsible for keeping everyone else safe.*
- *I don't matter.*
- *I'm invisible.*
- *I am not enough.*
- *I am not pretty.*
- *I am not okay.*
- *I am inadequate.*

- *I am worthless.*
- *I am less than others.*
- *I am better than others.*

If none of these descriptions is quite accurate for you, how would you state the lie or lies that have been planted in your heart? You may have already started to identify some of these beliefs as you worked through the earlier sections of this book—look back in your notes for any repeated patterns or hurts that came up in your answers. What are the words that repeat automatically in your mind? What thoughts immediately surface when you are in crisis?

Keep in mind that these beliefs are not always conscious, and they are rarely divulged to others. But these core lies often seem true at a gut level. While our minds may tell us they are not true—that they are contrary to what the Bible teaches—our throats, chests, and stomachs tell us something else. We react instinctively to people and events, behaving as if these lies were true. It requires prayer and focused effort to step outside these beliefs, to see that they exist in us, and to identify them as lies. Why is it so important that we identify these lies? Because we can't change them unless we first acknowledge them.

Step 3: Explore Their Impact

In addition to identifying the lies that have taken root in our hearts, it is important to discover how they have affected us.

What unnecessary pain or fear have they caused? How have they impacted our adult relationships? How did we cope?

Our coping mechanisms can bring as much or more pain to us than our original experiences with our mothers. Unhealthy coping techniques can introduce big problems into our adult lives. Sometimes, the ways we avoid pain can become ways we avoid life.

Here are a few examples of the many ways we cope:

1. **Becoming a People Pleaser**

   If a woman holds a belief that she is inherently flawed, unloved, or unworthy, she may become like a chameleon, putting on a persona to be acceptable to others but losing herself in the process.

   "If I was a 'good girl,' Mom would notice me," said Nina. "I didn't want to make trouble or argue with Mom like my brother did. It made her angry and dismissive toward him. I wanted her approval and attention. I got it when I came home from school with A's or washed the dishes. But hard as I tried, I could never be good enough to get the warmth or praise I wanted. She never really let me know I was okay.

   "When my dad left us, I was told to be a 'good little soldier.' I took care of my mom by pretending I had no feelings or needs. I didn't want to create any more trouble for her.

   "As an adult, the ingrained pattern continues. I am always putting my feelings and my needs aside to please others. I always have a smile on my face, and people think I'm nice. I avoid conflict and almost never say no. If there is a need—with a friend, at school, at work, or at church—I am always available to fill it. That may sound like a 'good' way to be, but it often comes at the expense of caring for my own family, my own health, or my own soul."

Many of us are people pleasers in some way. What would it look like to make it our goal to please God first and foremost?

2. Numbing Ourselves

When they can't stand the pain caused by the lies in their heads, many women turn to substances or activities to escape. Some may use drugs or alcohol. Some may overeat. Others may become workaholics or overindulge in romance novels, shopping, or television. Still others use busyness, social media, ministry work, or constant social activity to keep their feelings in check. While these types of solutions work in the short term, they can lead to bigger problems, such as addiction, broken relationships, or diversion from the life of purpose we were meant to live.

Victoria wondered why her mother was so cold toward her. "I could never get the hugs or 'I love yous' I longed for. I coped by going into my own fantasy world, making up songs and plays that would make me happy. Around age twelve, I discovered romance novels. They all had a similar plot: After initial rejection and struggles, the heroine would finally be seen as the beautiful, accomplished, amazing woman she was, ending up in the arms of the man who adored her. Reading these stories was comforting and gave me hope that things might get better someday."

Victoria entered marriage full of hope, but shortly after her first child was born, her husband was given a long-term, out-of-town assignment. "That was when my escape into fantasy got out of hand. I could not walk down the book aisle at Safeway without buying a gothic novel. I spent hours reading or watching soap operas. I'm ashamed to say there were times I ignored my son. It also hurt my marriage. No man could ever measure up to the fictional men that filled my mind."

We all have found ways to numb ourselves. What would it look like to run to God for comfort instead?

3. Excessive Dependency

Some women haven't developed the ability to take responsibility for themselves. Instead, they helplessly wait for someone to rescue them. This can be a response to being raised by a neglectful mom, who did not teach and guide them, or a helicopter mom, who did too much for them. It can also develop from having a critical or performance-oriented mother who caused the daughter to give up trying.

Sophia's mother wanted her to be brilliant and

gifted. As early as first grade, Sophia's mother would hover over her as she did her homework, correcting her mistakes, hoping to impress the teacher. Every time Sophia attempted something, her mother would correct it or improve it. As a result, Sophia eventually stopped trying.

One of her core lies became "I can't do things well enough." This belief spilled over into other areas of her life. When Sophia's mother signed her up for soccer, Sophia would not fight for the ball. She would stand back and let others do it. When it was time to apply for colleges, Sophia had her mother fill out the applications and write her essays. As an adult, Sophia continues the pattern of waiting for others, including God, to rescue her. Rather than setting goals and working toward them, she sits in her misery, hoping someone will bail her out.

Do you find yourself continually wanting others to rescue you or make things better for you? Could this be something that sabotages your growth?

4. Excessive Self-Reliance

Some women have been repeatedly hurt or disappointed by their mothers, and they come to expect that everyone else will also disappoint them. They fear that if they are vulnerable, they might be hurt, so they ultimately rely only on themselves. These women may find ways to distract themselves (work, addictions, fantasy) so they won't feel the loneliness that results from the lack of deep connection. They may choose similarly avoidant friends and spouses. Or they may have difficulty in their relationships because they hold others at arm's length.

Aisha said, "Around age seven, I started taking showers by myself. If I got shampoo in my eyes, I would call for my mom, and she would come and hand me a washcloth. On one occasion, when I cried out to her, blinded by the burning soap in my eyes, she responded coldly from the kitchen, 'You're old enough. Figure it out.'

"I stood there with my eyes tightly shut, terrified, feeling around for something I could use to put over my eyes and relieve the burning sensation. It seems like a small thing, but that incident solidified a message that has become my motto: 'Don't ask for help. Figure it out for yourself.' I learned that needing help meant I was weak, and it was shameful to be weak.

"In some ways this approach has helped me to be successful, but I often take it too far. If there are twenty-eight hours of work to do in twenty-four, I handle it. I carry the entire burden rather than seeking help, and it brings me unnecessary levels of stress. Also, I tend to isolate myself when I am feeling emotionally vulnerable, rather than reaching out to friends and family."

Do you find it hard to be vulnerable or to reach

out to others for help? What would it be like to have others support you and share your load?

5. **Becoming Controlling**

When we develop imprints that whisper to us that we are in danger of being left alone, criticized, or hurt, we may become controlling as a tactic to prevent those things from happening. We may think that if we can control our husbands, we can stop them from hurting us. If we can keep our homes and families in perfect order, we can calm the anxious voices inside us that suggest our world is chaotic. Control can be overt, like that of a drill sergeant, or it can be subtle and manipulative, like the woman who uses the "silent treatment" on others who don't do what she wants.

Nikki's mother had nine children and was usually distracted and exhausted. As child number five, Nikki felt powerless. She couldn't stand up to the bullying of her three older brothers or the bossiness of her older sister. She didn't have her own room or even her own socks. She never felt completely cared for or safe. When she went to college and only had one roommate, she seized the opportunity to have order. She wanted there to be rules about tidiness, when they could have guests, and when the lights needed to be off. At her core were unrecognized beliefs that whispered, "I am not safe. I don't have a place. I'm powerless." She compensated by becoming excessively controlling.

Do you find yourself trying to control your surroundings or other people? What would it look like to find your peace in God, instead of in your circumstances?

Underneath each of these coping mechanisms is an unmet need, a need that God longs to meet. He is always pouring forth his love and his truth, but our own faulty thinking—the lies that have cluttered the pages of our souls, making the truth illegible—causes us to rely on our own ways of managing life and relationships.

Speaking through Jeremiah, God rebuked the Israelites when they stopped relying on him and turned to their own devices:

My people have done two evil things:
They have abandoned me—
    the fountain of living water.
And they have dug for themselves cracked cisterns
    that can hold no water at all!

JEREMIAH 2:13

God understands that we were just children when our "cisterns" were established—our own ways of coping with loneliness, fear, or hurt. But now that we are grown, God wants us to rely on him to provide us with the living water we need.

A STARTING FOCUS

Ask God to help you focus on one area to start with. What is the core lie that resonates the most with you? How does that belief affect you? What strategies have you adopted to cope? How have those coping strategies helped you, and how have they hurt you? What is it that you specifically want to ask God to heal first?

As examples, here are our areas of focus and how we are seeking God's healing. This may seem redundant, but this exercise took each of us to a new level of conciseness and clarity. Healing is like peeling an onion; it often requires that we go over the same ground at a new depth.

- *Debbie: One lie I want to work on is that there is something wrong with me—that I am not enough. This thinking created deep insecurity from a young age and a drive to overachieve. As an adult, I have typically assumed it is always me who is "wrong" when there is a relationship problem. I quickly move to negative thinking about myself and apologize, even if I haven't done anything to warrant it. I have coped by walking on eggshells rather than facing my true fears of rejection. I believed I deserved to be rejected or treated unfairly. I want to replace this belief with the truth that I am enough and I am a woman of worth because God created me as I am. I want to be authentic in relationships and to love others without concern about myself.*

The core lie I believed: "*There is something wrong with me.*"

The ways I coped: Overachieving, people pleasing, self-blame, expecting rejection

- *Joan:* One lie I want to work on is that there is no one outside myself whom I can rely on. In the deepest parts of me, I sometimes feel like an orphan, anxious and alone. I have coped by being excessively self-reliant, by burying myself in busyness and achievement, and by isolating myself from others. I want to replace this imprinted belief with what I understand to be true about God—that he is always with me, guiding me and caring for me—and I want to be able to lean on him more. I also want to cultivate appropriate trust in others, to be more willing to reach out to them and ask them for what I need.

  The core lie I believed: "*I am alone and have no one to rely on.*"

  The ways I coped: Overachieving, avoiding intimacy, excessive self-reliance

Explore Your Story

1. Reread step 1 and write a prayer to God in your journal.

2. Momplicated Time Line: Get a large piece of paper and create a time line of your life up to the age of eighteen, focusing on your relationship with your mother— positive memories on the top part and negative memories on the bottom. You may want to use multiple pages. We have created an example of what this could look like on page 171.

3. Beliefs: Now go back through your time line and add beliefs that may have resulted from these entries. Don't overthink this; write the beliefs that pop into your mind. You can refine them later. You may find that one incident seems to bring up a lot of beliefs, or one belief may run through numerous incidents. You may want to use a different color pen for this. See how this was done in the same example on page 172.

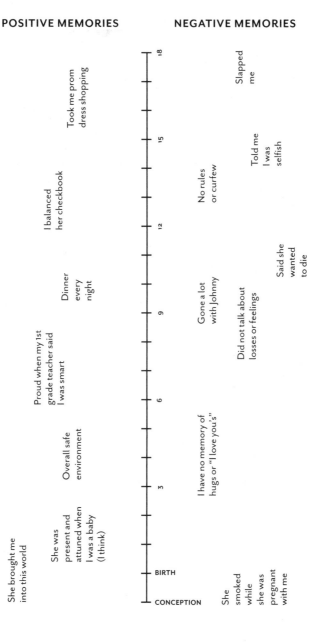

MOMPLICATED TIME LINE: *Key Events of My Childhood*

POSITIVE MEMORIES

NEGATIVE MEMORIES

She brought me
into this world

She was
present and
attuned when
I was a baby
(I think)

Overall safe
environment

Proud when my 1st
grade teacher said
I was smart

Dinner
every
night

I balanced
her checkbook

Took me prom
dress shopping

I have no memory of
hugs or "I love you's"

Gone a lot
with Johnny

No rules
or curfew

Slapped
me

Told me
I was
selfish

Said she
wanted
to die

Did not talk about
losses or feelings

She
smoked
while
she was
pregnant
with me

BIRTH

CONCEPTION

3   6   9   12   15   18

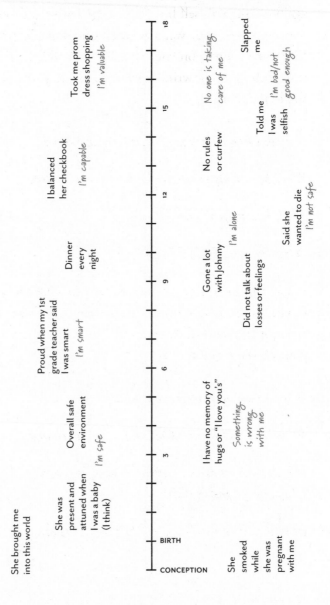

MOMPLICATED TIME LINE: *Key Events of My Childhood + Beliefs Instilled in My Heart*

POSITIVE MEMORIES   NEGATIVE MEMORIES

She brought me into this world

She was present and attuned when I was a baby (I think)
I'm safe

Overall safe environment
I'm safe

Proud when my 1st grade teacher said I was smart
I'm smart

Dinner every night

I balanced her checkbook
I'm capable

Took me prom dress shopping
I'm valuable

She smoked while she was pregnant with me

I have no memory of hugs or "I love you's"
Something is wrong with me

Gone a lot with Johnny
I'm alone

Did not talk about losses or feelings

Said she wanted to die
I'm not safe

No rules or curfew

No one is taking care of me

Told me I was selfish
I'm bad/not good enough

Slapped me

CONCEPTION — BIRTH — 3 — 6 — 9 — 12 — 15 — 18

4. Impact/Effects/Coping: Look back over your time line again, asking yourself how these experiences and beliefs have impacted you. What are their ongoing effects? Either make notes on your time line (possibly in a third color pen) or write in your journal as you consider these questions:

How did I cope with my experiences and beliefs?

What blueprints were laid for future relationships?

What habits were built into me?

What expectations did I take on?

5. Prayerfully look through your entire time line and ask God to reveal to you one particular belief or theme to focus on as you read chapter 10. You may want to ask yourself these questions:

What is causing me the most pain?

Which issue do I think God most wants to change?

Which patterns are most destructive to my current relationships and my life?

Write that area of focus in the following format:

One core lie I have believed is . . .

The ways I have coped are . . .

You may also want to write the new belief and behaviors
you want to adopt:

The truth I want to believe is . . .

The new ways I want to act are . . .

Connect with God

*Lord, it is hard for me to admit, even to myself, the core lies I
have held tightly and believed all these years. It is even harder
to admit some of the coping patterns I have developed that are
not healthy for me or the people closest to me. As I open my
heart to you in this area, I am asking you to do a deep and
lasting healing. May your Holy Spirit penetrate my emotions
and transform me in ways I could never do on my own. May
every memory that you bring back to my mind be covered with
grace, truth, and healing. I desire to walk in the truth of your
love for me and be reshaped by you. Amen.*

10

healing continues
by living in the truth

*I have no greater joy than to hear that
my children are walking in the truth.*

3 JOHN 1:4, NIV

WE BEGAN OUR INNER healing journey in the previous chapter by discussing these initial three steps: (1) pray; (2) identify core lies; and (3) explore their impact. In this chapter, we will look at the final three steps that will help lead us into the abundant life God has planned for us.

Step 4: Apply God's Truth

To heal, we must change our thinking. Scripture teaches us that our lives will literally be transformed by the renewing of our minds (see Romans 12:2). I (Debbie) learned a lot of Scripture after becoming a Christian, but I later realized that what I had learned in my head had not traveled to the depths of my heart. My negative view of myself as a result of my relationship with my mother was rooted deep. Instead of applying the truth of God's Word to my real life and hurts, I was studying the Bible for knowledge. I memorized verses, but they didn't change the way I lived. The music of my soul was made up of despondent chords. Maybe that is why this quote resonates with me:

> There is a difference between memorizing Scripture and thinking biblically. There's a difference between knowing the words and experiencing their meaning. There is a difference between having the sentences embedded in your head and having their impact embedded in your heart. . . . There is a difference between "doing Christianity" and *being* a Christian. You can memorize all of the words, but if you've forgotten the music, or never experienced it firsthand, then you still won't be able to sing the song with fullness.[1]

I grew up singing and know what it's like to forget the music. It's a vulnerable feeling. In the same way, when we forget the music of God's love for us, we are vulnerable and often stuck in the wrong thinking of our past. We might confess that we are new creations in Christ, but we don't live like it. At a conference for the American Association of Christian Counseling, Sandra Wilson summed it up well: "We don't always live what we profess, but we always live what we believe."[2] That is why it is so important for us to look at the core lies we learned through our relationships with our mothers—and to bring those beliefs to God for change.

As we've mentioned, the healing process isn't a quick fix—rewiring our habitual thinking requires attention that often can seem overwhelming. But be encouraged: God will walk with you every step of the way.

It is often said, "I know it in my head, but how do I get it in my heart?" The authors of *The Common Made Holy* gave a helpful picture of the process:

> Imagine that your mind is like a pitcher that was intended to be filled with crystal-clear water, but it got contaminated with coffee over the years. One day you decide you want the water in the pitcher to be pure, but are saddened upon discovering that there is no way to get the coffee out. Then you discover nearby a bowl of crystal-clear ice cubes, which is labeled, "Word of God." There is no way you can pour the whole bowl of ice cubes into the pitcher at once, so you drop in one ice cube a day. At first the task seems hopeless, because the coffee is so pervasive. Slowly, however, the daily infusion of truth eventually nullifies the effects of the coffee. Then finally comes the day when the coffee can no longer be seen, smelled, or tasted even though a remnant of it is still there. Likewise, that process

of renewing our minds *will* work provided that
we don't pour in a tablespoon of coffee for every
ice cube.[3]

What core lie did you identify at the end of the previous chapter? If that lie is the coffee that contaminates your pitcher, what biblical truths will be the purifying ice?

For example,

- *If your mother was critical, and your core lie is that you are not good enough, find Scripture that helps you see yourself through God's eyes, such as Psalm 139:14: "Thank you for making me so wonderfully complex! Your workmanship is marvelous—how well I know it."*

- *If your mother was detached and cold, leading you to a core lie that you are not lovable or worthy of celebration, hear God's love for you in Zephaniah 3:17 (NIV): "He will take great delight in you; in his love he will no longer rebuke you, but will rejoice over you with singing."*

- *If the environment your mother provided left you with a constant sense of anxiety and fear, begin adding ice cubes of truth like Psalm 61:3: "You [God] are my safe refuge, a fortress where my enemies cannot reach me."*

As the example of the pitcher and ice cubes shows, change may be slow, but it still requires our direct participation.

Inner healing happens when we live remembering the heart of God rather than staying stuck in our own thoughts. The Holy Spirit, whom Jesus called the Spirit of truth, makes the truth known to us, embedding it deeply in our souls:

> I will ask the Father, and he will give you another Advocate, who will never leave you. He is the Holy Spirit, who leads into all truth.
>
> JOHN 14:16-17

> When the Spirit of truth comes, he will guide you into all truth. He will not speak on his own but will tell you what he has heard. He will tell you about the future. He will bring me glory by telling you whatever he receives from me.
>
> JOHN 16:13-14

Danielle sat in silence as she remembered the times her mother had asked, "What's wrong with you? Why are you so sensitive? Why can't you shake things off?" With each memory of her mother's glower, she felt a surge of insecurity. She also recalled the times when her mother would flippantly say that she loved her, but Danielle didn't believe that her mother even liked her. As a result, Danielle had learned to question herself and be ashamed of who she was. She knew that God's Word said Jesus loved her, but it didn't move her. She was stuck.

After prayer and reflection, Danielle knew what needed to happen. She asked the Holy Spirit to make the truth of God's love real to her at a heart level. As she took what she believed about herself and held it up to what God believed about her, everything began to change. Slowly, she let the truth into her hurt places, and her mother's words eventually became a faded backdrop in her story, rather than the reality that kept her hating and shaming herself.

Ask the Holy Spirit to replace the lie you have believed with God's truth. Find verses that refute the lie. You may want to circle them in your Bible, write them on three-by-five cards, and memorize them. Though we cannot fully understand this dynamic, the Word of God is alive and powerful.

The word of God is alive and active. Sharper than any double-edged sword, it penetrates even to dividing soul and spirit, joints and marrow; it judges the thoughts and attitudes of the heart.

HEBREWS 4:12, NIV

All Scripture is God-breathed and is useful for teaching, rebuking, correcting and training in righteousness, so that the [woman] of God may be thoroughly equipped for every good work.

2 TIMOTHY 3:16-17, NIV

Jesus is our example. When tempted, he called out Scripture, claimed it, and based his actions and choices on it. In the same way, we have the power of the Holy Spirit working in us to refute the lies and call out the truth, claiming it as our very own. The Holy Spirit will bring us everything we need for healing.

If this process is new to you or something you haven't done for a while, here are some practical ways to begin:

- *Write out the Scripture. Something happens when your hand holds a pen and puts down the words on paper.*

- *Repeat the Scripture. Choose a time to remind yourself of the verse. For example, at the top of each hour, recite it again to yourself.*

- *Use your voice. Saying or singing Scripture out loud is powerful.*

- *Listen to songs that have Scripture as lyrics.*

- *Pray the Scripture. Thank God for the promise and ask for it to be fulfilled in your life and your relationship with your mother.*

- *Journal the Scripture. What does it mean to you at this point in your healing journey?*

- *Rewrite the Scripture in your own words, draw a picture, or write a poem that captures what it means to you and your relationship.*

- *Process the Scripture with a trusted friend or counselor.*

- *Thank God in advance for rewiring your emotional self with his truth.*

For me (Joan), it has been powerful to remember, personalize, and recite to myself Bible verses that directly refute my false beliefs. When everything in my gut brought back the old beliefs from my relationship with my mother that said, *I am all alone,* I would remind myself of the truth: *Jesus' name is Emmanuel—God with me. God said he would never leave me nor forsake me. In him I live and move and have my being. The Spirit of Christ lives in me.* I would acknowledge that the verses didn't *feel* true at the moment, but I knew I could choose to believe the Bible rather than what my feelings were telling me.

Slowly, God's truth began to feel more and more real. When a person would appear in my life at just the right time or my prayers would be answered, I no longer saw those things as luck or happenstance but as the involvement of the living God who was always present and watching over me.

When my (Debbie's) mother was older and came to live with us, the momplications were often more than I could handle. It was then that I knew I had to do something to survive my day-to-day life and interactions with her. I wanted to hold on to the truth that God had been teaching me, but my relationship with my mother was testing my faith. After recognizing that I needed to be strong in God's love, I began to reflect and remember truths from Scripture by setting the alarm on my sports watch to signal me hourly.

Each hour I would breathe this prayer: "Thank you, Jesus, that you know me and that you value me. You know the situation I am in, and you are with me." This repetition centered me so that when I would arrive home from work, I was much more willing to act in that same love toward my cranky mother. "Thank you, Jesus, that you know my mom and you value her. Help me to value her too."

Before long, I began to change. When my mom was negative toward me, there was a new grace in how I interacted with her. Why? Because I was purposefully remembering the truth. This practice only took seconds every hour but paid dividends too large to measure.

Why is it so important to do these things? Because there is a war raging in our minds. The apostle Paul gave these instructions to the believers in Corinth, but they are equally true for us today:

> We are human, but we don't wage war as humans do. We use God's mighty weapons, not worldly weapons, to knock down the strongholds of human reasoning and to destroy false arguments. We destroy every proud obstacle that keeps people from knowing God. We capture their rebellious thoughts and teach them to obey Christ.
>
> 2 CORINTHIANS 10:3-5

Strongholds are patterns through which incoming information is processed.

> When we give place to the enemy's *lies* for any length
> of time, it's as if we have made an agreement that
> these lies *are* true. These lies can become *strongholds*
> in our soul for him to set up shop and torment us.
> Most of the time we won't even realize what has
> happened. He has gained *topography* in our hearts,
> minds, personality, or intellect, and we cannot
> free ourselves because these lies now have a *strong*
> *hold* on us. . . . When we filter things through past
> hurts, rejection, and painful experiences, it becomes
> impossible to believe God and accept his love and
> faithfulness.[4]

Step 5: Acknowledge the Good

As I (Joan) look back through my life, I can see a long line of women God has used to fill in the gaps my mother unknowingly left in me. These women have taught me life skills, emotional skills, and relational skills. They have listened to me, encouraged me, and challenged me. Most important, they have taught me about God and how to develop a relationship with him.

My mother was never able to show me the way to overcome suffering, but God has sent me women who have. There have been personal friends like Diane, who, like my mother, lost her son to leukemia, but became stronger as she drew closer to God. There have been women I have met through their books, like Corrie ten Boom, who experienced God's presence while in a Nazi concentration camp. I have heard the testimonies of women like Joni Eareckson Tada, who was paralyzed from the shoulders down, yet grew stronger in her faith as a result. These women have put flesh on the Scripture I read, assuring me that God is always with me and will work all things together for my good (see Romans 8:28). Their stories challenge my old beliefs that there is no God, that no one is in charge, that I am alone, and that life has no purpose—helping me rewrite those beliefs.

Do you believe God is always at work in your life? Do you believe he always has been? As you explore your momplicated past, can you see evidence of his divine hand?

Carmen struggled with deep emotional pain from a sense of feeling unloved, but she was unable to fully connect with the "why" of that pain. God impressed her to take out childhood photos of herself and put them on a bulletin board. She began praying in front of that bulletin board for the little girl in the pictures. Soon she began to remember her childhood in enough detail to realize why she grew up feeling unloved.

For Carmen, what seemed like a crazy idea at first turned out to be God leading her to the core lie that needed to be changed. Then the truth began to set her free. God showed her that he had always loved her, kept her safe, and been in every chapter of her personal story. His truth began to flood her mind: "I have cared for you since you were born" (Isaiah 46:3). As Carmen looked at the images of her young self, internalizing that truth, she began to deeply feel God's compassion and love for the little girl in those pictures. God's love became real. It was more than a verse to hold on to; it was a relationship with God as the parent she had always longed for.

Some women have to admit the hard truth that they have no memories of their mothers showing them love. If that is true for you, God is waiting for you with open arms. He offers to bind up your wounds and fill your empty places.

We (Debbie and Joan) have both good memories and bad. Most women, when asked to describe their mothers, do so with a mix of positive and negative statements, such as "I don't remember her ever hugging me, but she worked hard as a single mom to support our family," or "She was depressed and spent a lot of her time in bed, but I know she loved me very much." The majority of us have received both hurts and gifts from our mothers, and both need to be examined for us to see the whole picture.

We've spent a lot of time looking at the ways our mothers did not meet our needs. Now let's see if we can find ways they did. What are the gifts your mother gave you? At the very least, every mother gives her daughter life. She was the person through whom you entered this world. She carried you inside her womb, and her body fed your body.

Even with momplications, some women will easily find positive memories about their mothers. Others, however, will have a harder time. In order to completely heal, we need to be open to telling ourselves the full truth. In the end, our goal is to move beyond the negative and focus on what is good, hopefully in our mothers, definitely in God.

> Whatever is true, whatever is noble, whatever
> is right, whatever is pure, whatever is lovely,
> whatever is admirable—if anything is excellent
> or praiseworthy—*think* about such things.
>
> PHILIPPIANS 4:8, NIV, EMPHASIS ADDED

The word translated *think* is the Greek word *logidzomai*, which means "to consider or calculate." The NASB uses the phrase "dwell on these things." This is not a fleeting thought of a Bible verse or a happy memory but an intentional, deep reflection that enters our hearts and affects our actions. When we focus on any good that our mothers brought to our lives, we are lining our thoughts up to God's desire that we dwell on the good. As we cultivate gratitude, we open our hearts up to love, healing, and a new perspective.

Pray for a softening of your heart and understanding for your mother. Ask God to show you his hand in your past and in your present. As you pursue healing, look for practical glimpses of his love and care for you. Be open to nudges from him to take action. God will often allow situations in our lives that we don't understand or welcome, but the reality is that he may be pulling out our weeds of distrust and uprooting the unhealthy messages that have tainted our hearts. Trust the process and cling to his promise: "If you look for me wholeheartedly, you will find me" (Jeremiah 29:13).

Step 6: Live Out of Your Spirit-Led Self

Are you beginning to grasp what it looks like to align your mind with the truth of God's love? It's a relationship that God has always wanted to have with you. In the past, you may have responded to life in ways you learned as a little girl. Old triggers may have dictated your reactions and hampered your relationships. "When I was a child, I spoke and thought and reasoned as a child. But when I grew up, I put away childish things" (1 Corinthians 13:11).

God wants to grow us into our mature, Spirit-led selves. Living in the Spirit means you are free to love God, others, and yourself rather than being in bondage to old coping mechanisms that make you defend, control, or withdraw. And though we once lived as our mothers' children, we are now learning to live as God's children.

Marla wasn't invited to a family birthday party.

And though she understood it was a small, intimate

gathering of her brother's immediate family, she felt hurt and left out. She realized for the first time that this default reaction resulted from old wounds, a sensitivity to feeling left out as a child. She stepped back and asked God to help her look at the situation objectively. The truth was, she really wouldn't have wanted to travel the distance to the party, and her brother knew it. God made it clear, so that Marla could see it with an adult perspective. This breakthrough only happened when she moved beyond her childish reactions.

Walking in the Spirit is learning to rely on God's love for you—learning to live as his daughter rather than living in the broken pieces of the past. When we begin to embrace God's love, we also learn to assign that love to others.

Because we are his children, God has sent the Spirit of his Son into our hearts, prompting us to call out, "Abba, Father." Now you are no longer a slave but God's own child.
GALATIANS 4:6-7

We know and rely on the love God has for us. God is love. Whoever lives in love lives in God, and God in them. . . . There is no fear in love.
I JOHN 4:16, 18, NIV

Have you been afraid to let others in? Perhaps it's your mother you have trouble loving. Living by faith means letting go of the past and processing things from a different perspective. Each day you really do have a choice—to react like the little girl who was wounded (the flesh) or to respond like the free and new woman you are in Christ (the Spirit). Sometimes you just have to "faith it until you make it"—walking in faith according to what is true and right rather than living according to your feelings, which are subject to your broken and still-healing places.

What are the differences between living in the self and living in the Spirit?

- *The self-led life includes these reactions:*
  "hostility, quarreling, jealousy, outbursts of anger, selfish ambition, dissension, division" (Galatians 5:20)

- *The Spirit-led life looks like this:*
  "love, joy, peace, patience, kindness, goodness, faithfulness, gentleness, and self-control" (Galatians 5:22-23)

Jessica jumped at every opportunity to quarrel with her mother. Her mother had irritated her when she was a child, and now that she was an adult, this irritation grew to outright hostility. Nothing her mom did was ever right. What Jessica really longed for was peace with her mom; she just didn't know how to find it. A committed Christian, Jessica began to realize that all the quarreling and hostility was coming from her own negative thoughts. She was living in her flesh, but she desperately wanted to be a woman characterized by walking in the Spirit.

Over time, Jessica realized that with every irritation, she had a choice. The more healing she found for the hurts of her past, the more she could freely choose to follow the Spirit's leading. Slowly her irritation and aggression were replaced with compassion and peace. Ultimately, this choice affected not only her mother-daughter relationship but all of her relationships.

What would your relationships with others, including your mom, look like if you were Spirit-led? Imagine living out of the fullness of God's Spirit:

- *You trust God with his plan, rather than trying to control all the pieces of your life.*

- *You acknowledge when your emotions are triggered and go quickly to God.*

- *You approach situations with more trust than suspicion, and you tell the truth even when a lie feels safer.*

- *You declare the truth of God's Word rather than listening to the lies of the enemy.*

- *You choose to reach out to others rather than becoming isolated from people.*

- *You give to others even when you feel forgotten.*

- *You refuse to feel sorry for yourself and instead remember things you are grateful for.*

- *You open your heart to love, acceptance, and forgiveness.*

We believe these wise words from A. W. Tozer: "Get Christ himself in the focus of your heart and keep him there continually. Only in Christ will you find complete fulfillment. Throw your heart open to the Holy Spirit and invite him to fill you. He will do it."[5]

Explore Your Story

1. Find one verse that refutes the lie you identified in chapter 9. Using the verse as inspiration, write an affirmation of truth that you can hold on to. For example, "I'm his treasure" (based on Deuteronomy 7:6).

2. Write out a list of characteristics of God's love from 1 Corinthians 13:4-7. This will help you learn God's heart toward you. This is not a list of what we are to do

but a list of the aspects of love we are receiving. It may look something like this chart:

GOD'S LOVE	HOW THIS CHANGES ME	MY CHILDHOOD VIEW OF LOVE
Love is patient.	God knows my imperfections and yet still loves me.	I need to try harder and get it together to earn my mother's love.

3. Find one or more pictures of yourself as a child. As you look at them, tell your younger self all the characteristics of God's love you have discovered in 1 Corinthians 13:4-7. Ask God to show you the ways he was there for you even then.

4. Reflect on the fruit of the Holy Spirit in Galatians 5:22-23. Make a list and ask God to bring those peace-inducing, life-giving characteristics into your heart. Journal about how you, as a child, would have benefited from receiving each one of them from your mother.

Connect with God

Lord, we have been on an amazing journey since day one. You have seen everything that has shaped my belief system, formed my habits, and influenced my view of life. I know now that

I have been holding on to lies that have kept me self-focused and insecure. I want you to perform a miracle in me that only you can do. Make your words of truth life-giving realities in my soul, and heal the unhealthy places in my heart. I desire to walk in your Spirit and put away childish ways of coping, reasoning, reacting, and responding to life. This is possible with you. Amen.

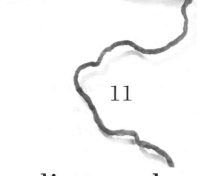

11

healing can happen in your current relationship

Your success ... is fully determined by how powerful you are willing to become. Will you become a person who can keep your love on, no matter what? A powerful person says, "I am going to be okay no matter what you do. You can hurt me, but you cannot make me turn my love off."

DANNY SILK

MOTHER'S DAY WAS A WEEK AWAY, and I (Joan) stood in front of a rack of greeting cards. I picked up one after another, but none of them seemed quite right. Some were sappy and sweet with sentiments like "You're the sunshine to light my day." Other messages simply were not true descriptions of what I felt about my mother, like "You are an exceptional, inspiring woman, and I want to be just like you." I had a family of my own in California, and my mother still lived in Illinois. We had friendly phone conversations every Sunday, but she was not my sunshine and I did not want to be just like her.

What about you? Maybe you don't even bother reading those cards—or maybe you avoid the greeting card aisle altogether. For some women, a more honest card might say,

"Mom, even though your erratic behavior over the years is likely the source of my low self-esteem, biting sarcasm, passive aggression, and pervasive abandonment issues, I still really love you and hope you have a wonderful Mother's Day."

As adults, almost all of us want a close, connected, and satisfying relationship with our mothers—and not just on Mother's Day. We wish that our mothers, our very first friends, would now be among our best friends. But that does not—and should not—always happen.

As we've discussed, your inner healing is always possible through the power of the Holy Spirit. However, restoring your external relationship with your mom is not fully under your control. She must also participate if the two of you are to relate in open and loving ways.

Hailey was forty-three the first time she stood up to her mother. She and her husband had agreed to set boundaries for their twenty-two-year-old son, requiring him to get a job or move out of their house. Hailey's mother thought this was ridiculous and invited her grandson to come live with her. That's when the cold war began. Hailey's mother stopped inviting her to family events, including Christmas and birthdays. Hailey isn't sure why her mother shut her out. Was it because she ignored her mother's advice? Was it because her mother wanted the primary role in her grandson's life? For whatever reason, Hailey's mother treats her with scorn and rejects any of Hailey's attempts to talk or work things out. After two years of pain and trying to resolve things with her mother, Hailey has had to accept the fact that she cannot change her mother. For now, she no longer reaches out to try to make a connection.

It takes discernment and courage to determine how far your mom is able and willing to go with you in the healing process. If she has passed away, all that remains is for you to heal internally. However, while she is living, only God knows what possibilities exist to improve this important relationship. Take every step God offers to bring love and instill harmony in your relationship with your mother. Be diligent to do your part:

Do all that you can to live in peace with everyone.
ROMANS 12:18

If your mother does not do her part, your next goal is acceptance. Stop protesting, complaining, trying to fix her, or hoping she will be all you want her to be. Extend grace to her. When you think of her, pray for her. Let God be in charge of the journey, whether or not she changes.

THE SERENITY PRAYER

Have you ever heard this familiar prayer?

> *God, grant me the serenity*
> *to accept the things I cannot change;*
> *courage to change the things I can;*
> *and wisdom to know the difference.*

Look closely and you'll see three requests combined in one, asking God to help you with things you cannot change, things you can change, and things you are not sure whether you can change:

1. *The things you cannot change:* What are the things that you cannot change about your mother and how she relates to you? Perhaps she is unwilling to address certain issues because she doesn't want to hurt you by discussing them or she doesn't feel strong enough to face them herself. Perhaps you have asked her to talk about your history together, and she has refused. Perhaps you are realizing that she is narcissistic, that no matter what you say or do, she focuses only on herself and her needs. Perhaps she has dementia or has died, leaving no hope for resolution with her. When

you come to the point where you are clear you have done all you can, then pray for the serenity to accept those particular things about your mother that you cannot change.

2. *The things you can change:* What other actions could you take? Perhaps you need to open a discussion, write a letter, or set a boundary. When you identify these things, pray, "God, grant me the courage to _____," filling in the blank with each specific action you sense might be the right, good thing to do.

3. *The things you're uncertain about:* Maybe you are hesitant, wondering if you should push for change or just leave things alone. You may be asking, "Should I speak up and confront her? Or do I just need to accept her as she is?" In these cases, you don't know whether to pray for the serenity to accept or the courage to act, so ask God for wisdom to know the difference. Then wait and listen for God to show you which way to go.

Which part of the Serenity Prayer stands out to you? Remember that no matter what your mother does or does not do, you can walk in God-given grace and power as you seek to live in peace with her.

A HEALING CONVERSATION

I (Debbie) thought my mother would change once she became a Christian. She did change in many ways, and our relationship improved. But there was always an underlying angst between us. Because of this, I never stopped trying to please her. Even in our dysfunctional dance, we spent lots of time together. When I married and had a family of my own, she was attentive and encouraging to her grandchildren. To others, everything looked good, but behind closed doors she was mean and condescending to me. Our unhealthy relationship kept me off balance.

By 1991, my mom, a widow with multiple health issues, could no longer live on her own. My husband graciously invited her to come and live with us in our downstairs guest room. I had mixed feelings about the arrangement, but I followed my husband's loving lead and held on to the verse about honoring my mother. I trusted God would help us live peacefully under the same roof. Almost immediately, our new living situation confirmed that something was still very wrong between the two of us.

It was a push-and-pull existence, with both of us trying to take the lead. In front of the family, Mom was pleasant enough toward me. But when we were alone, she snapped at me and criticized me, and when I would call her from work to check on her, she often hung up the phone abruptly. I often found myself holding back tears.

And then it happened. I got the call that my mother had suffered a second major heart attack and was in intensive care.

After conferring with doctors, it was clear that she had to undergo open-heart surgery involving all major arteries and all feeder arteries—a surgery that the doctor wasn't sure she would live through. After my sister, Sharon, and I prayed for her and comforted her, she was taken to the operating room. The two of us spent the day at the hospital, waiting nervously—pacing, crying off and on, and continuing to pray. My relationship with my mother was far from ideal, but I didn't want to lose her. I was terrified that she would die without my ever knowing why things had been the way they were between us.

Will I ever know what has been wrong all these years?

Why was she close to Sharon but always seemed to hold me at arm's length?

What was it about me that made her irritated and argumentative?

Why did she reject me when she could see I needed her?

Did she really ever love me the way I loved her?

Thankfully, she made it through the surgery and then came back home to live with us. Once home, my mother continued to be hard on me. This was confusing because she was well-liked by everyone else. She had charisma and could be the life of the party, was a generous gift giver, and was an amazing Memaw to her grandkids. She was kind to my husband and volunteered on prayer teams, caring deeply for the people she prayed for. Yet, despite her relationship with others, we still had a dark cloud hovering over the two of us. My children noticed it too. "Why is Memaw so mean to you?"

A counselor I had been seeing encouraged me to have the tough conversation with my mom when she got well enough. One night when I was alone with her, I nervously broached the subject.

"Mom, there is something wrong between us. You seem fine with everyone in the family except for me. It doesn't matter what I do—it's always wrong. This has gone on my entire life. We are two adult Christian women who need to sort out this problem.

"When you were in surgery, I was afraid that you would die and I would never know what was wrong—what was wrong with me . . . why couldn't you accept me? Why did you always say I messed up when I was trying so hard to be good? Why didn't you treat me the way you treated other people?"

As she turned her face away from me, her bottom lip began to quiver and tears trickled down her cheeks. "I have never wanted to tell you this . . ."

She then began to tell me the saddest story—her story.

"I was eighteen when my mother died, and when I met your father and fell in love, it numbed the pain. Somehow I didn't realize that my new husband was an alcoholic. When Sharon was born, I was busy taking care of her, hoping your father would stop drinking. Instead, it got worse. I began to secretly plan a way out. For a few years I hid money from our monthly budget. I figured that when Sharon was a teenager, she would be able to help by working a part-time job. Together, we would make it on our own.

"Then I found out I was pregnant with you."

The tears now were streaming from her eyes as she continued. "I never wanted you. You spoiled my plan, and I resented you for that. I believed you had ruined my life. When I began to have complications early in the pregnancy and was put on bed rest, I resented you even more. I was stuck with you and my marriage."

She paused for a moment. "And then you were born. When I heard your first cry, my heart instantly changed. My anger and bitterness were overcome by love for you. I was sure everything was going to be okay.

"But it wasn't. Once we got home, you cried and screamed each time I held you, but you quieted down whenever you were in the arms of your sister or your drunk father."

My mother's next words pierced my heart.

"You rejected *me*," she said. "Maybe you were punishing me for my bitter thoughts toward you when I was carrying you. Whatever the reason, it was more than I could bear. I was not going to let you hurt me. When you were about six months old, I made a decision. As a strong Catholic, I felt that God had brought you into my life, so I promised God that I would raise you and provide you with every physical need, but I would not let you into my heart."

She had kept that promise. I'd had everything I ever needed, except the warmth, snuggles, and love of my mommy. She had successfully kept me at arm's length, walled out from her heart, and I had spent my life feeling that my own mother didn't like me. But . . . God knew. He had planned for my birth.

This healing conversation happened when I was in my forties and Mom was in her seventies. She apologized to me in tears.

"How could you ever forgive me? Do you think I didn't see what a good girl you were? How you tried to get my attention? I just couldn't give it to you; I had vowed not to let you in. If I let you in, you would hurt me, just like your daddy had hurt me with his drinking. Besides, your daddy loved you enough for us both."

That day was our new beginning. I held my frail mother in my arms, and we both wept for the years we had lost. Then we promised to make the rest of our years count. It wasn't perfect, but I did get many "I love yous." A few months before she died, she even told me something I had never heard from her. She said I was pretty. After the first time she said, "You are so pretty," she repeated "pretty, pretty, pretty" over and over again. It was a moment I will never forget.

We had a couple of good years, and when my mom was placed in hospice care, we had lots of time together. One day while I was by her bedside, she whispered, "Why did I wait so long to tell you I really did love you? Why did I waste that time?"

As I wiped away her tears and mine, I assured her, "It's okay, Mom. We are here now, and it's enough. I will always love you; you are my mommy."

Not a day goes by without my thinking of her. Tears are falling on the keyboard as I type this and remember her. My love for her is deep.

And this is the part that fascinates me today. God knows our stories. He has observed each page being written, and he desires for us to bring each pain-filled paragraph to him. When I began to realize my life was part of God's bigger story of redemption, my pain began to have a purpose.

If there is a chance that your mother might be open to change, begin praying about how to initiate a discussion with her about your relationship. Some mothers are fully willing to engage and resolve issues. Others want to open up, but they have a natural defensiveness. To bring up the past is a risky thing. Why address issues that seem better left alone? For those of us in painful or uncomfortable relationships, being brave enough to have an adult-to-adult conversation with our mothers will help us move forward both emotionally and spiritually. Pray for courage and an attitude of love, not blame. The goal is not to hurt your mother but to let her know your experience and then to listen and understand.

How can you confront your mother without slipping into the blame game? Consider using the following format: "When you _____, I feel _____. I want _____." For example, "Mom, when you frequently criticize my weight, I feel hurt and discouraged. I want you to accept me as I am."

Keep in mind that your mother today is likely different from the woman who raised you. She has probably matured and learned some things. Some of us have an ugly image of our moms frozen in our minds that we continue to hold on to. We need a new picture that represents who they are today, to see them with fresh eyes through a healing lens.

Here are some practical questions to ask yourself when considering a conversation of healing, closure, or understanding with your mother:

- *Have I been bringing my own hurts to God for healing?*

- *Am I looking for peace, or am I trying to hurt her?*

- *Can I address my hurts without blaming her?*

- *Can I listen to her, understanding that she isn't perfect?*

- *Am I willing to move forward without an apology from her?*

- *Am I willing to accept her for who she is, not who I wish she would be?*

- *Am I open to forgiving her even if she doesn't understand how badly she's hurt me?*

The true battle is not between ourselves and the mothers who have hurt us; it is between our histories and our best possible selves. When we are willing to relinquish the urge to fight one more battle with our mothers to gain their recognition, acceptance, or admiration, then we are ready to move forward and heal. As we've done throughout the book—and especially in chapter 10—we must always work to yield ourselves to God, ask him to re-parent us in the areas where our mothers fell short, and live under the power of his Spirit.

There is no guarantee that your mom will respond positively to your attempts at resolution. She might refuse to talk, or she might change the subject. She might say you are making things up, that your memories are false. She might tell you that you are too emotional or too sensitive. She might not show you any empathy, and she might never say she is sorry. She may act as if you have wounded her, rather than taking responsibility for hurtful things she has done. She may listen politely but continue in her dysfunctional ways. These responses would be disappointing but not surprising. Pray for God to help you accept her as she is. Then rest in the knowledge that you have obeyed God and have done your part to try to heal the relationship.

WHAT COMES NEXT: NAVIGATING THE RELATIONSHIP

What if you have done your part to heal your relationship with your mother, but her response has been disappointing? How do you proceed? How do you move forward as a Spirit-led woman? It is a challenge to love the unlovely, to honor someone who is not acting honorably, or to serve someone you may need to protect yourself from. To do this, you must honor your mother and also set appropriate boundaries.

Honor Your Mother

It is one of the Ten Commandments, the first one mentioning our relationship to another human being:

Honor your father and mother. Then you will live a long, full life.

EXODUS 20:12

But how can we truly honor our mothers, knowing our relationships are full of painful momplications, some of which may never go away? We must give our mothers these three gifts: love, acceptance, and forgiveness.

1. **Love:** The way to love your mom is to be first filled with God's love yourself. You cannot give what you have not received. Love is who God is, and we can only love others as his love flows through us. It is not always easy. But by the power of the Holy Spirit within us, we can be patient when our mothers are difficult, kind when they are demeaning, and always hopeful that God will transform them. Jesus taught that we are to love even our enemies and pray for them. How much more should we each show love to the one who brought us into the world?

   Love is patient and kind. Love is not jealous or boastful or proud or rude. It does not demand its own way. It is not irritable, and it keeps no record of being wronged. It does not rejoice about injustice but rejoices whenever the truth wins out. Love never gives up, never loses faith, is always hopeful, and endures through every circumstance.

   I CORINTHIANS 13:4-7

2. **Acceptance:** Accept your mom by giving up the dream that things could have been different. Release any need for her to be the mother you always wanted. We realize this is not easy and may need to be done repeatedly. When you are hurting because of your unmet needs, ask Jesus to meet you in the pain. Acceptance may mean that you will have a polite, superficial relationship with your mother and that you will need to go to God and other people to have your needs met. As unfair as it may be, you may never hear the things you need to hear from her; you may never get the love and nurturing that you desire. Be willing to lower your expectations so you do not continue to get hurt each time you reach out, hoping for different results. To accept her is to show grace for who she is right now, in all her flawed humanness. Jesus models this. He accepts and meets people right where they are. He welcomed and loved prodigals, tax collectors, and prostitutes, not waiting for them to change before he had a relationship with them.

> Accept each other just as Christ has accepted you so that God will be given glory.
> ROMANS 15:7

3. **Forgiveness:** Forgive your mom by releasing any right to punish her or take revenge for the ways she has hurt you. That is God's business, not yours (see

Romans 12:19). You are not excusing her for what she did—you are choosing to treat her with love. If you hold on to resentment and are unwilling to forgive her, the only person you are hurting is yourself. It has been said that unforgiveness is like drinking poison and expecting the other person to die. Jesus offers forgiveness to everyone for the wrongs they have done, and we are taught to do the same. In fact, Jesus made it clear that we are forgiven as we forgive others.

> Since God chose you to be the holy people he loves, you must clothe yourselves with tender-hearted mercy, kindness, humility, gentleness, and patience. Make allowance for each other's faults, and forgive anyone who offends you. Remember, the Lord forgave you, so you must forgive others.
>
> COLOSSIANS 3:12-13

Set Boundaries

Loving, accepting, and forgiving your mother does not mean you must surrender your boundaries with her. Boundaries are a part of every healthy relationship. Ideally, relationships are a balance of loving others and loving ourselves. Boundaries are one way we take care of ourselves. They are a way to say, "I'm me. I have my own identity. I am responsible for myself and my choices. I have my own thoughts and feelings. I have a right to say no. There are times I should not allow myself to be mistreated."

Boundaries can be especially tricky for mothers and daughters because initially their identities were intertwined. Many of us can set healthy boundaries with other people, but somehow we don't feel we have the right to set them with our mothers. Yet, every daughter needs to step into her own identity; she needs to be responsible for her own interior world, her own safety, and her own choices. The choices you make about how and when to set boundaries are between you and God. They depend on your values, your culture, and how the Holy Spirit is leading you in each situation. Just remember that God is your ultimate authority, even above your mother.

Here are four ways we might set boundaries with our mothers:

1. *Just say no.* The word *no* is sometimes all that is required to set a boundary. "No, I'm not going to talk right now." "No, I won't be visiting you this weekend." "No, you may not take my child to that movie."

   For example, Caroline loves her mother dearly and enjoys spending time with her, but she feels burdened by the amount of time and attention her mother wants. Because her mother complains that she is lonely and has no other friends, Caroline feels guilty whenever she says no to her mother. However, when Caroline's husband expressed his frustration that they couldn't do anything without her mom, Caroline realized that she needed to set some boundaries for the sake of her marriage. She needed to let her mother be responsible for herself and cultivate other relationships. She needed to sometimes say no.

2. *Speak up.* Speaking the truth in love is usually a right and necessary first step toward resolving a difficult issue. This is assertive communication—kindly, clearly, and confidently stating your request. To determine whether or not to talk to your mother about a particular issue, ask yourself which of the three parts of the Serenity Prayer applies. Is this a time to remain silent and pray for the serenity to accept her as she is? Is it a time to pray for the courage to speak up? Or do you need to wait and pray for wisdom? If you sense that speaking up is the right thing, your prayer for courage will help you move past the fear that you might not get a good response. Remember that you are not responsible for her reaction. Even if your mother responds poorly, you will have the calm assurance that you have done your part to resolve things.

That proved true for Claudia. Her mother had a habit of going through Claudia's drawers and closets when she visited, organizing and discarding things she did not think were worth keeping. Claudia sat down with her and said, "I appreciate your desire to help, but please don't go through my things anymore." Her mother was hurt and embarrassed, but she respected her daughter's right to be responsible for her own possessions. Claudia let go of the resentment she had been feeling, and her relationship with her mother improved.

3. *Take action.* When a discussion has not brought about change, it may be necessary to take action. Some actions are small, like deciding not to share vulnerable thoughts or feelings with a mom who is unable to validate you. Other actions are more extreme, like excusing yourself and going home when she is saying or doing hurtful things.

Imagine if Claudia's mother continued to go through Claudia's things, despite numerous requests for her to stop. Claudia would need to take her boundaries beyond words. She might need to install some locks or stop leaving her mother alone in her house.

4. *Set internal boundaries.* Internal boundaries are ways we protect our minds and our emotions from outside influences. They may take the form of self-talk that refutes harmful messages coming in from the outside: "Mom just said I was stupid, but I'm not," or "Her body language is telling me she doesn't approve, but I know I am doing the right thing." Another form of internal boundary may be the refusal to absorb the emotions of another person: "Mom is almost vibrating with stress. I'm going to breathe and stay calm."

A third type of internal boundary might be resisting being pulled into old, familiar patterns: "I can see that you are trying to be the helpless victim and get me to rescue you, but I'm not going to play that game."

Helen's mother often made mean and critical remarks to her. She had spoken to her mother about this, but to no avail. Yet she loved her mother and wanted to have peace with her as far as it depended on her. She prayed for the serenity to accept her mother and for the ability to give love in return for the prickly barbs she received. She also prayed for God to protect her heart from the pain she experienced while she was with her mother. She imagined Jesus physically standing between her and her mother whenever they were together. Jesus shielded Helen and absorbed her mother's barbs. Helen was aware of them, but they did not hurt. As a result, she could respond to her mother with kindness rather than reacting angrily.

5. *Stop communicating.* Sometimes speaking with or being with your mom is so painful or toxic that you need to cut off communication. This is an extreme and difficult decision, but at times it can be necessary for your well-being.

Tabatha knew something needed to be done. At twenty-three, she had already spent years working with a therapist to overcome the effects of her alcoholic mother's abuse and neglect. She loved her mother and longed for the rare times when her mother was sober and kind to her. However, it was usually drunk, mean, manipulative Mom who would show up when they got together, leaving Tabatha devastated and barely able to function for days afterward. With her therapist, Tabatha decided to write her mother a note that said, "I love you, but until you get into recovery for your alcoholism, I cannot be around you. I will no longer respond to your texts or calls." Tabatha had to protect herself from her mom by creating this boundary.

When Mom Is in Need

The Bible tells us that we should care for those who are in need, especially family members. Jesus rebuked the Pharisees for instructing people to give money "to God" rather than caring for their own parents (see Mark 7:9-12). Paul used equally strong words: "Those who won't care for their relatives, especially those in their own household, have denied the true faith. Such people are worse than unbelievers" (1 Timothy 5:8).

It can be difficult to discern how to appropriately apply this principle in today's world. Is it okay to put Mom in a nursing home? Is it okay to say you will help her financially or with household chores but not allow her to move in with you? What if you don't have the resources to help her? How do you balance her needs with the needs of your husband and children? When is it time to say yes, and when is it time to implement boundaries?

We may resolve this dilemma in a variety of ways. As my (Debbie's) mother's health declined, it was clear that she could no longer live alone. She didn't ask to move in with us; it was something that God put on my husband, Ray's, heart. After seven years, she required hospice care and moved to my sister's house. She spent the remaining months of her life there.

God led me (Joan) to help my mother in a different way toward the end of her life. My sister, my aunt Betty, and I rotated, staying with her for a week at a time. God provided people to care for my children and the resources to fly across the country, and it felt like the right thing to do. Years later, I did the same thing for Aunt Betty. She was a widow with no children, and I didn't want her to be alone. So I spent the last two months of her life with her at her home in New York.

In the end, our job is not to obey every request and whim of our mothers, but to seek God's will for how to love and honor them and then faithfully obey him. This can truly be a momplicated situation, which may require the help of a pastor or counselor. Don't be afraid to seek out professional advice to help you navigate complex circumstances.

When Mom Is No Longer with Us

When my (Joan's) mother turned seventy, she was diagnosed with an autoimmune disease and emphysema. A few months later, her kidneys failed and she was hospitalized. There she descended into a gray depression, spending long days gazing blankly at the wall of her room. Fearing she might be dying, I prayed fervently that she would come to know the

God who had done so much for me. When I tried to share my spiritual journey with her—how lost and alone I had felt when Daddy and Johnny had died, but how God had helped me feel connected and hopeful—she only heard the pain in my story and, with grief on her face, said, "I know. I wish I had gotten you some kind of help." Despite my prayers and my attempts, she was never open to spiritual conversations.

In December of that year, I was in Alabama for my brother-in-law's funeral when my sister called to say our mother had slipped into a coma. I arranged to catch the next plane to Chicago. I begged God to give me one more chance to speak to my mother. I had recently heard a woman say that the love of God had been revealed to her while she was in a coma through a friend's playing worship music, reading Scriptures, and speaking to her even though she was unconscious. I wanted that same opportunity with my mother. I believed I had fallen short in my attempts to explain God's love and needed another chance. I still had hope. I desperately wanted to see a happy ending to our story!

As I sat in the middle seat on the airplane to Chicago, praying my heart out, I suddenly knew it was too late. Somehow, supernaturally, I knew my mother was gone. I picked up the phone on the back of the seat in front of me and called the hospital. The nurse put my sister on the line: "She just died, Joanie."

Sitting on that airplane, tears pouring down my cheeks, I asked God the same questions I had asked at age nine when he didn't move my pencil: "Why couldn't you do this for me,

God? Are you real? Do you care?" The temptation to bitterly reject him again was huge, but I couldn't do it this time. I had too much history with him. God's words came to mind: "As the heavens are higher than the earth, so my ways are higher than your ways and my thoughts higher than your thoughts" (Isaiah 55:9).

Even though the last few months with my mother were sweet, and she remarked on how "nice" I had become, I did not feel that her story on earth had a happy ending. But I remind myself that I don't know the whole story. Maybe God heard my prayers and met her in that coma. Maybe I will see her in heaven and we will joyfully fall into each other's arms. Or maybe not. I don't know how her particular story will end, but I choose to trust in God's goodness. So I release her to him, realizing that his mysteries are beyond my comprehension . . . and all is well with my soul.

Many of us are healing from wounds that cannot be addressed in this life because our mothers are gone. We cannot rewrite the stories of our mother-daughter relationships, but we can rewrite the script of our own stories, allowing God to redeem our pain and heal us from the disappointment that things did not turn out the way we wanted.

Though we cannot bring our mothers back, there is still a way to move forward: We can grieve with hope. How do we grieve with hope? We look back and remember the good as well as the bad of our relationships with our moms and acknowledge all the feelings that arise. We also look up and remember the God who redeems all things. We remind ourselves that this life isn't all there is, and we can hope in an eternal future when the pain of this life is gone. We remember the bigger picture of God's sovereignty over our lives. He enables us to pass through the pain, forgive our mothers, and let go.

Remind yourself of these truths:

- *You are precious and lovable.*
- *You can have a life of happiness, peace, and joy (soul abundance in Christ).*
- *You can be treated with respect.*
- *How others treat you is a reflection of who they are, not who you are.*
- *You can live a rich, full life, even without the outcome you hoped for.*
- *The only approval you need is from God.*
- *There is an awesome, wonderful future awaiting you—a bigger story.*

Explore Your Story

1. Do this Serenity Prayer exercise:[1] Divide a blank piece of paper into three columns. At the head of the first

column, write "Things I cannot change." At the head of the second column, write "Things I can change." At the head of the third column, write "Not sure." Then think about anything that might be troubling you about your mother, and list your thoughts in the appropriate column. Here is an example:

THING I CANNOT CHANGE	THINGS I CAN CHANGE	NOT SURE
God, grant me the serenity to accept these things.	*God, grant me the courage to do something about these things.*	*God, grant me the wisdom to know which of the other two columns this item belongs in.*
I cannot make my mother go to therapy and work on her insecurities.	I can pray that God will lead her to a place where she finds healing.	I'm not sure whether I should suggest therapy to her or not.
I cannot stop her from smoking.	I can ask her not to smoke in my house.	Is it okay for me to ask her not to smoke when I'm in the car with her?

Now use this paper as your prayer guide, praying for serenity, courage, and wisdom. As you think of new things or receive wisdom, feel free to add, change, or move items. This is meant to be a working document.

2. Make a list of every positive thing that comes to mind about your mother. Reflect on what was or is true, honorable, right, pure, lovely, admirable, excellent, or worthy of praise about her (see Philippians 4:8).

3. Write your mother a letter that expresses all your true thoughts and feelings—the joys and disappointments of your relationship with her. Be open and honest. This is for your eyes only. After you write it, read it aloud—to a trusted friend, to an empty chair that you imagine your mom sitting in, or to God. Then destroy the letter as a symbolic act of letting go of all your hurts and resentments.

4. List your own wrongs, resentments, and hurtful actions toward your mother over the years. Consider meeting with her to ask her forgiveness.

5. Ask God to show you ways you can honor your mom.

6. Pray about creating healthy boundaries with your mom. What would that look like? What actions might you need to take to establish those boundaries?

7. If your mom is willing, set a time to meet and discuss moving into a better relationship.

Connect with God

Lord, you know every part of my heart and story. You have clearly instructed me to love, accept, forgive, and honor my mother. This is hard when the painful memories come back to me, but I trust your leading. Help me to see the good in her, letting go of the bad that I have held on to. Give me your love and acceptance for her, and as I move into that kind of love, enable me to love myself as you love me. This healing path is all about freedom and living in truth. I commit my heart and mind to you now, and as hard as it may be, I commit myself to the path of honoring, loving, forgiving, and healing. Have your way in my life, Lord. Amen.

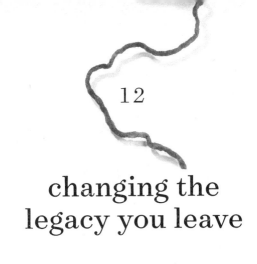

12

changing the
legacy you leave

We will be known forever by the tracks we leave.

ANONYMOUS

HERE WE ARE, AT THE END OF our journey with you, hoping that you have found something valuable in these pages. We tried to ask relevant questions, suggest helpful exercises, tie in Scripture, and tell relatable stories—information and insights to make life less momplicated for you. We are certain you have worked hard; maybe you had to take breaks every so often to catch your breath or dry your eyes. Maybe there were times you stopped and didn't think you'd finish. The truth is, after you read the last word in this book, your real journey begins.

The stories of our lives unfold as we walk down our own paths. Since the moment you were conceived, your mother has shaped you. Her love or inability to love is woven into the fabric that defines who you have become. Regardless of how we as daughters began our journeys, one thing is certain: We, too, are adding texture and meaning to the fabric of the lives that come after us. We are difference makers in the lives of our daughters, granddaughters, stepdaughters, nieces, and others, and the differences we make will go on for eternity. Whether we have biological children or not, we all leave a legacy.

Who will teach the next generation how to heal? How to hope? How to love? How to be a woman of integrity and faith? We will. And we will do it not only with words but with the very essence of who we have become as God's daughters. Remember, we are leaving heartprints—our unique stamp on everyone we encounter. Healing isn't just for us. It's for those who follow us.

Do others see the love of God in us? Have they experienced him in our choices to love, accept, and forgive? How we love, how we hope, and how we live our lives are the very things that we pass on. We are not expected to be perfect, but rather imperfect women who look to God. Sally Clarkson, in her book *Own Your Life*, described the significance of a mother's impact:

> Mothers, I came to believe, were God's finest idea
> for how such a righteous legacy would be passed on
> in each generation. They were designed by Him to
> influence the hearts of children within the sanctuary

of their own homes and to help shape them into the next generation of godly leaders. Mothers have the capacity to inspire messages of truth and hope, to model love and servant leadership, to build mental and academic strength by overseeing the education of their children, to lead in faith, and to build a haven of all that is good, true, and beautiful.[1]

The goal of this book has been to lead us to a point where we can stand in the truth of our restored lives, regardless of our pasts. When we do this, we experience increasing freedom in Christ. It is this freedom that we pass on now, this grace and truth that we hold out to our children and their children. We are women who have been hurt or even completely broken, but despite it all, we have never been abandoned by God. This is a new day. We are giving future generations a new place to stand.

When we lean on God and walk in truth, we break the bondage of what might have been a long line of generational dysfunction. We change the legacy we leave by changing the only thing we can—ourselves.

We are intricately involved in the process of shaping destiny:

Whoever sows a thought, reaps an action;
Whoever sows an action, reaps a habit;
Whoever sows a habit, reaps a lifestyle;
Whoever sows a lifestyle, reaps a destiny.[2]

Each of us stands at a pivotal point in our personal histories. Our smallest choices lead us either toward God or away from him, toward love and truth or away from them. Every choice we make is like a pebble thrown into a lake that sends ripples out in all directions. What is the ripple effect of your life?

WE CAN BE THE TRANSITION GENERATION

Several years ago, I (Joan) traveled with my sister, Annie, to our grandmother's hometown to visit the site where our grandmother, mother, and aunt were buried. It was a drizzly, overcast day when Annie and I picked our way through the mud to the far corner of the garden next to our grandmother's church. There, engraved on a low stone wall, we found the dirt-streaked names of the three women who had been so important to us—the matriarchy that had raised us.

As we stood there, a memory flashed into my mind. I was sitting at my grandmother's kitchen table eating Wheat Chex and grapefruit when she suddenly announced, "I've bought a small plot where my ashes can be buried. It's in a nice shady corner of the church garden. I also bought two extra spots for anyone else in our family who might want to use them."

I had been an oblivious teenager back then, and now I wished I could go back and spend one more night at her house and eat one more breakfast with her. I would tell her how much I loved her and how important she was to me. I would treasure her every word and ask her to tell me more about herself.

I shared those thoughts with Annie, and we stood silently, engulfed in our sadness as we missed all three of them.

The quiet was broken by Annie's words: "Will you pray?" Her request caught me by surprise since she had always described herself as "not religious."

I took both her hands and prayed out loud, thanking God for our grandmother, mother, and aunt, and all they had poured into our lives. I thanked him for how much they each had loved us in their best-that-they-could-do ways. I knew that more than anything, they would have wanted us and our children to have good, blessed lives—lives that were even better than theirs had been. I knew that there would have been no better way to honor them.

The words of one of my graduate school professors came to mind. She would often say to us, "You can be the transition generation." So that is what I prayed.

"God, please let Annie and me be the transition generation—the generation that stops the negative trends in our family and starts positive ones. Let this prayer today be a spiritual line in the sand. Let it divide the past from the future. Give us the power to change things for the better."

Annie joined me, and we went back and forth, speaking our requests as they entered our minds.

"God, help us talk about things instead of burying our heads in the sand and staying stuck. Please let us and our children acknowledge our hurts so they can be healed."

"The women who are buried here all experienced abandonment or unfaithfulness in their marriages. Let future marriages in our family line be faithful, loving, and long-lasting."

"God, the women in our family have tended to give up and accept defeat in many circumstances. We ask for courage so that we and our children can be fighters who persevere and overcome the things that stand in our way."

And on it went . . .

I have seen answers to many of those prayers since that day. Fifteen years later, Annie received a cancer diagnosis and was told she had only three to six months to live. She responded with courage and strength and became all the more true to who she wanted to be. She never buried her head in the sand. Instead, she encouraged friends and family to talk openly about their feelings, and she did the same with them. She died with no unfinished business. I have no doubt she made her peace with God.

Like Annie and me, my daughters are deeply committed to authenticity and growth. Now that they are adults, we are companions on this healing journey, often laughing about the less-than-perfect ways I raised them or talking about the dysfunctional patterns we share. Whether it be how we relate to men, or body image issues, or the pressure to achieve, our conversations usually help us all grow in understanding and closeness. We are still far from perfect, but I'm grateful that my healing, even at this late stage, helps them. This note from one of my daughters is on my refrigerator:

Happy Mother's Day, Momma!! I want to be just like you when I grow up. Thank you for being my biggest supporter, always a phone call away, the all-around best mom—always willing to grow, change, and laugh. I love you more than all the stars in the sky!

That message blesses me more than I can say. My mom did the best she could. So did I. None of us is perfect, but we can move beyond our pasts into a better future—one of hope and healing. Our wounds truly are the windows through which God's light can shine.

$\sim$

Perhaps you have a different story and have been rejected by your own daughter (or someone who is like a daughter to you). Maybe you wish she would invite you to lunch, respect you for the wisdom of your years, or thank you for the love you have poured into her. You long to leave a positive legacy, but for now at least, it is out of your hands.

We would like to remind you of three things:

1. *One of the best things you can do for those who come after you is to heal yourself.*
2. *Apply the Serenity Prayer exercise from chapter 11 to find wisdom for how to proceed.*
3. *Remember that your story is not over yet.*

LIVE LIKE IT'S REAL

Like Joan, I (Debbie) know that my mother had a good heart and did all she could with what she had. Unlike Joan, I never knew my grandparents and wasn't close to any of my aunts. My female influence and modeling came mostly from my mother, and all I learned about our family came from the stories she told me of alcoholism and tension between siblings. All of these things shaped me, because all of these things shaped my mother. And though there were years of pain between my mother and me, the last years were rich with love. In the end, the woman who hurt me the most left me the greatest legacy.

My sister and I, with the help of hospice workers, cared for our mother until the end of her life. Early one Monday morning, after weeks of a steady decline, the hospice nurse encouraged me to talk to my mom about letting go. As hard as it was to tell her we would be all right, I knew it needed to be done.

"Mom, we are at peace with your leaving us. It's okay."

She searched my face, waiting for me to say more. After a few moments of silence, she defiantly said, "Well, I'm not going anywhere without you and the boys!"

She had a special bond with her grandsons from living with our family all those years, and the love was mutual. I paused, thinking about how she was present, oxygen tank and all, at every Little League game that my boys played. When my older son got his license, he'd drive my mom to the mall to get her hair done, escorting her in her wheelchair. We would certainly miss her.

Taking a breath of courage, I leaned in a little closer. "Mom, it's your time to go, not ours."

"That's easy for you to say. I'm going alone, and I just hope everything we believe in is real."

The look of fear in her eyes broke my heart. Although she was a Christian, she was clearly afraid to die, so I began to pray that God would bring her peace in a real way.

She slept most of the week until Friday morning. My sister, Sharon, called to tell me I should visit Mom earlier rather than later, so I rushed across town to Sharon's house and climbed the stairs to Mom's room. The minute she saw me, she smiled—the biggest smile I had ever seen on her face.

"Debbie, it's so fancy there!" she exclaimed with childlike excitement. I had never heard her use the word *fancy* before.

"Where, Mom?" I asked, quickly making my way to her side.

"Sit down, and I will tell you all about it." As I sat next to her, she began to describe the angels she had seen and other glimpses of heaven. "There are emeralds as big as boulders, and the streets shine like glass." She was most intrigued that there seemed to be "appointment times" for each of us to get in. For the next half hour, she "painted" a picture of heaven for me. Her mind was sharp and clear as she filled in detail after detail.

The nurse, who was sitting in the corner of the room with tears in her eyes, whispered to me, "She's not on any meds. These are not hallucinations—this is real!"

When Mom was done pouring her story out to me, she made a quick shift. "I'm ready to go!" she declared. Just like that—from fear to faith—she was ready!

I marveled that this was the same woman who, days earlier, wasn't going anywhere without me and the boys, and now she seemed excited to go. With urgency she said, "Go get the boys. I want to say good-bye."

I phoned my sons, waking them up on a lazy summer morning, telling them to be ready to jump in the car when I got home. My mind was an emotional blur, but I did my best to explain to them what had just happened. The three of us arrived and gathered in her room.

Like me, my two boys love to sing, and Mom loved to hear us. She asked us to sing her favorite worship song, "Beautiful," one last time. As we sang, I noticed her smiling and nodding as if she were acknowledging others around the room.

When we finished, she said, "Oh, you sound so much more beautiful with the angels."

Justin, my oldest, said, "Grandma, it's just us here."

"Oh no, this room is filled with angels."

She motioned for him to come closer. "Justin, you have always been Grandma's big blond boy. I have never wanted to leave you. But you know those angels that it talks about in the Bible? They're real. I've seen them, so I don't have to worry anymore. You're safe. Just promise Grandma one last thing before I go . . ."

My son could barely get the words out between his sobs. "Anything, Grandma, anything."

"Justin, live like it's real . . . because it is."

He hugged her gently as his brother, Cameron, slipped in next to her. "Cameron, you are such a good boy, and Grandma doesn't want to leave you. But now I know there are angels who will watch over you. Promise me one thing before I go."

He made the same promise that Justin did. "Anything, Grandma, anything!"

"Cameron, live like it's real . . . because it is."

The boys huddled in the corner together crying, and she motioned for me to come.

I could see Mom was getting tired. She pulled on my collar, bringing my face right up to hers. Her faded brown eyes looked stern and serious.

"Debra . . ."

Uh-oh. She only called me Debra when I was in trouble.

"Debra, live like it's real . . . because it is."

I was weeping so hard that I couldn't speak, but I managed to nod.

She had one last charge. "And those women you speak to? Tell them to spend their lives living like it's real."

There was no final "I love you" from my mother, but I received a greater gift in those four words: "Live Like It's Real."[3]

Those words gave me a new lens with which to view life. Though I miss her more than I could have ever imagined, I remember her by keeping the promise I made at her bedside. I close every one of my speaking engagements with the last words she spoke. With our hurts behind us and eternity in front of us, we were just two imperfect women who longed for God in our everyday lives. My mother left me a charge, and now I leave it wherever I go as well.

How do we live like it's real? By looking up and embracing a story much bigger than us. By staying in the truth, connecting to God daily, and asking the Spirit of God to have his way in us. How do we pass it on? By walking it out, as imperfect women, loving others through the perfect love of the almighty God. As I write these words, I think of the trail I will leave, lovingly picturing the little girls and women in my family now—my granddaughters, stepdaughters, daughters-in-law, and nieces. I want them to live out of whole hearts, believing that the truest thing about themselves is that they are loved by God.

Love the LORD your God with all your heart and with all your soul and with all your strength. These commandments that I give you today are to be on your hearts. Impress them on your children. Talk about them when you sit at home and when you walk along the road, when you lie down and when you get up. Tie them as symbols on your hands and bind them on your foreheads. Write them on the doorframes of your houses and on your gates.

DEUTERONOMY 6:5-9, NIV

God's Word is to be

- *Pressed into our hearts*
- *Passed along to the next generation*

- *Talked about along the journey*
- *Remembered in as many ways as possible*

THE BIGGER STORY

As you have discovered the areas where you may have been hurt by your mother, hold on to the hope that whatever was lacking in your mother can be found in a loving God. In chapters 5 through 8, we looked at four needs that a mother ideally will fill for her daughter. Let's look at how God meets those needs for you:

- *God is always present. Human mothers are limited. Much as they may want to always be there for their children and be attentive to their needs, circumstances arise that take them away, either physically or emotionally. But the Holy Spirit is able to remain with us in every place at every moment. With the Holy Spirit, we are never alone.*

  > I will ask the Father, and He will give you another Helper (Comforter, Advocate, Intercessor—Counselor, Strengthener, Standby), to *be with you forever.* . . . He (the Holy Spirit) *remains with you continually* and will be in you.
  >
  > JOHN 14:16-17, AMP, EMPHASIS ADDED

- *God is our safe place. Our mothers may not have been able to protect us. The truth is, none of us is guaranteed complete safety in this world. Jesus told his disciples, "In this world you will have trouble." But he also said, "I have overcome the world" (John 16:33, NIV). This life is fleeting, but we are offered an eternal safety. Our souls are safe in God.*

> The LORD is my rock, my fortress, and my savior;
>   my God is my rock, in whom I find protection.
> He is my shield, the power that saves me,
>   and *my place of safety.*
>
> PSALM 18:2, EMPHASIS ADDED

- *God leads, guides, and teaches us. Our mothers may not have stepped up to do these things, but we have been given the Bible and the Holy Spirit to lead and guide us in the life choices we make now.*

> The LORD is my shepherd. . . .
> He *guides me* along right paths . . .
>
> PSALM 23:1, 3, EMPHASIS ADDED

- *God celebrates us. Our mothers may not have let us know they valued us for who we are, but we have assurance from God that he loves and cherishes us. The message from heaven that was spoken over Jesus at his baptism is whispered to us by the Holy Spirit:*

You are my beloved daughter, whom I love,
in whom I am well pleased.

SEE LUKE 3:22, EMPHASIS ADDED

Jesus knows our mothers did not always meet our needs, and he longs to fills those empty places in our hearts—so that we can be made whole and so that we can share that richness with others. When we fear and serve the Lord, we lack nothing (see Psalm 34:9). We are given everything we need to live a life that leaves a legacy to all who know us.

By his divine power, God has given us everything we need for living a godly life.

2 PETER 1:3

Where will you go from here? Will you continue to acknowledge the reality of your momplicated past? Will you invite God into the broken places so that you can live from your Spirit-led self? Will you do your part to have the best possible current relationship with your mom? We hope you will join us in our heartfelt prayer—that at the end of our lives we will be able to say,

I have fought the good fight, I have finished the race, and I have remained faithful. And now the prize awaits me—the crown of righteousness, which the Lord, the righteous Judge, will give me on the day of his return.

2 TIMOTHY 4:7-8

Explore Your Story

1. What bad habits or negative patterns have been passed down to you that you do not want to pass down to another generation? Pray over each issue, asking God to stop the hurt and dysfunction from continuing through you. Ask God to use you as a "transition generation," so that through you, a new cycle of healing and wholeness will begin in your family.

2. Write a letter to those you have parented, especially your daughters, telling them the things you want them to know and remember when you are gone. You may want to acknowledge and apologize for ways you now realize you have wounded them. You may want to highlight generational patterns that you hope they will partner with you to change.

3. Write your own eulogy. How do you want to be remembered? What would you like people to say about you after you die?

4. How would your words and actions change if you began to "live like it's real"?

Connect with God

*Lord God, you have been with me since my first breath, and
you will be with me when I take my last. Throughout my life,
I have been shaped by hurtful messages, but you will never
fail to love imperfect me. Today I stand on the promise of your
Word, that what you have begun in me will be completed.
Your work will be done in and through me, and when I meet
you face-to-face, I pray you will say to me, "Well done, daughter. You have been a good and faithful servant." I believe this is
possible because of your power and grace. I now receive healing
to live beyond any mother wounds I have experienced. I will
be a woman who walks in love until the day I die. I will be a
woman who lives like your love is real, your Word is truth, and
there is more than just this life. Thank you for empowering me
to pass on love to those who come after me. I pray for all the
people whose lives I touch, that the love of Jesus will go deep
within their hearts and be lived bravely through their lives.
Amen.*

Q&A with Debbie and Joan . . .

Real people with real questions about real issues with their mothers and daughters.

I hate talking to my mom because when I hang up the phone or leave the conversation, I never feel good about myself. She always interrupts me, and there are times I can detect she's not listening to what I'm saying. I can't safely go to my mom with my problems and actually feel heard and helped, so I've learned to just shut down and say "Everything's fine" when she asks me about my life. She's astonished that we're not close, but how can we be when she doesn't listen to me or really see me? How can I be loving in these moments?

It's hard to have a mother who isn't a good listener. No matter how old we are, we all long for attunement from Mom—we want to know we are seen and heard. Yet our mothers are real people who may not have the ability to listen well. You say you never feel good about yourself after talking to her. What is the core belief about yourself that gets triggered? Maybe it is "I don't have value" or "I'm not important." Whatever it is, acknowledge it, and then ask God what he would say about that belief. The more you can soak in the reality that he sees you, hears you, and values you, the less your conversations with your mom will hurt. You will be able to let her actions be more about her than about you. Knowing and experiencing that you are loved and known by God, you will be more able to extend love and grace to your mom in all her imperfection.

Have you tried shifting the focus of the conversation at the moment you feel unheard? To do this, change the topic from whatever you were talking about to your mother's behavior. For example, "Mom, just now when I shared something that was important to me, you ignored what I said and went on to something else. I felt unheard and unimportant. It made me want to shut down."

If catching her in the moment is not comfortable for you, pray for courage and plan a time to have an honest conversation with her. It sounds as if she wants to understand why you are not close, so she may be interested in having this discussion. Be sure to tell her that you love her and that your motive is not to make her feel bad, but to have a close relationship. Also, be sure to give specific examples. You will need patience and God's compassion for her and for yourself. Even if she expresses a desire to change, she will not do it overnight.

I have a great relationship with my mom, but I'm
currently in a marriage crisis and she's the only
one I haven't told. I don't want her to worry about
me, and even more, I don't want her to turn against
my husband. My mom would be devastated if she
knew I was going through something so painful
and I wasn't letting her walk through this experi-
ence with me. What do I do? How do I know when
the time is right to talk to my mom, and how do
I approach it in a way that helps me and doesn't
hurt her? Am I wrong to have kept this from her
for so long?

Even in the most loving relationships, not everything needs
to be shared. You have stated two legitimate reasons why
it might not be wise to disclose your marital crisis to your
mother, at least right now. First, you don't want her to worry.
It is true that mothers often feel deep pain or fear when their
daughters are going through something difficult. Maybe
you believe this will be too heavy a burden on her. Or perhaps you are concerned you will need to emotionally care
for her at a time when you are already so stretched. Second,
you don't want her to turn against your husband. It can be
difficult for a mother to hear how her son-in-law has hurt
her daughter and not hold resentment toward him. Your
concerns are valid. During this time of crisis, you need to
take care of yourself and rely on supporters who can stay

emotionally grounded and who can cheer for the marriage, not just take your side.

Perhaps as you read this, you realize that your mom does have the capability to manage her own worries and to forgive and accept your husband. If so, then you may want to go to her now and openly tell her the concerns that kept you from sharing sooner, while expressing your confidence in her. Alternatively, if there is any reason that telling your mom now will add to your burden—even if it is just your inability to not worry about her—then please wait. This is a time to heal yourself and your marriage. We imagine that, ultimately, that is your mother's greatest wish.

My mom is constantly oversharing about different parts of her life (sex, money, personal issues, and frustrations with my dad and siblings). I don't want to know most of this information! Since there's no indication she is going to change, can you suggest a healthy way to get her to stop these personal discussions? And if not, what's the best way to respond when she brings this stuff up?

Maybe your mother doesn't realize how inappropriate her sharing is. Try having a conversation with her that is kind but firm, letting her know that you don't want to talk to her about these personal subjects. If she continues to bring them up in conversation, be a broken record, repeatedly saying, "Mom, please don't talk to me about . . ." until she gets the message. If she still ignores you, you may have to set stronger boundaries like leaving the room or politely hanging up the phone.

Can you suggest ways for me to continue a thriving and growing relationship with my adult daughters? How can I initiate conversations with them that encourage them to open up to me? Are there universal things that we can do to cultivate a deeper relationship during this stage of life? After all, this stage is a lot longer than when they're kids.

An important thing to remember with your adult daughters is that your role has changed. It's time to give the primary responsibility for their ongoing parenting over to God. A common complaint grown-up daughters have about their mothers is this: "Anytime I tell my mom anything, she tells me what to do or gives me advice." It is no longer your job to solve their problems. Instead, listen well, validate their feelings, and let them be responsible for their own lives. When they share their struggles, give responses such as "That's a tough situation. What options are you considering?" or "You are strong, and I know you will figure this out." Show them the same respect you would any other adult.

To encourage your daughter to open up, listen, listen, listen, and show understanding. Try inviting her to speak by asking a few open-ended questions, but if she shows unwillingness to talk, avoid grilling her. One wise mom found that if she sat on the couch and knit, her teens would gravitate to her when they wanted to talk. If you have a history of not listening well, you may have to wait for your daughter to let down her walls and share. Grab that opportunity to display your best listening skills.[1] Be silent, respectful, and openhearted until she finishes speaking. Rather than jumping in with your thoughts, reflect back what you heard, especially any emotion she has expressed. "Sounds like that was hard/embarrassing/scary . . ." Try to see things through her eyes, even if you don't agree with her thinking. Avoid giving advice unless she asks for it. Avoid making it a teaching situation until after she feels fully heard.

Beyond that, be your daughters' biggest cheerleader. Celebrate them for the unique people God has made them to be. See past their current imperfections to who they are becoming. The world will give them plenty of criticism and correction, but you can be the person who makes them feel deeply known and unconditionally loved.

Be authentic with your daughters, but remember that you are still their mom. Try to balance enjoying time with your daughters with cultivating other relationships, so you don't lean too heavily on them. Invite, don't guilt. Offer opportunities for fun times together, but allow them to say no. If you sense hurts or resentments in either of you, bring them into the open so they can be healed.

Most of all, enjoy and be grateful for your daughters.

They are imperfect, just as you are, but a mom's relationship with her adult daughter can be one of the biggest blessings in life!

My daughter has made it clear that she thinks my husband and I favor our son over her. We really tried hard not to do that. We believe we treated them very much the same as we raised them. Sometimes it seems as if nothing is ever enough. How do I help her understand that we really were doing our best?

Push the pause button on trying to convince her of anything and invite her to share her reasons for believing you prefer your son over her. Listen with openness and curiosity. Hopefully, she will be able to get to the root of her belief, possibly one or more memories that hold this belief in place. The incidents she relates may seem small or illogical to you. You may want to defend yourself or tell her you had good intentions, but stop yourself and just listen to her. Avoid minimizing ("That was silly") or defending ("We didn't mean it that way"). Instead, validate her experience with statements like "That must have been hard," or "I can see why you would have felt that way." Apologize for anything you may have done or said, even if you had the best intentions at the time, and reassure her that you love her. The more you can create a safe space for her to explore her memories and feelings, the more likely it is that she will find healing as you walk alongside her. If this is difficult for the two of you to do alone, a third party such as a therapist could be very helpful.

When is a mother allowed to speak up about things in her daughters' lives? Are you allowed to express your opinions, or do you just have to accept and support all their choices?

It takes wisdom and discernment to know when to speak up and when to bite your tongue. Of course, you are always "allowed" to speak up and express your opinions, but ask yourself what effect your words will have. Remember that every good relationship is built on respect. You don't have to agree with your adult daughter's choices, but we suggest you respect her right to make them. Expressing your opinion to your daughter by saying, "I think you would be making a mistake by taking that job, but I'm here for you no matter what you decide to do" is very different from trying to control her by saying, "Don't take that job." A good rule-of-thumb question to ask yourself is "What would I say to a friend, and how would I say it?" Another tactic that shows respect is to ask, "Do you want my thoughts or advice on this?"

How do you learn to communicate with each other when you have very different styles of communicating and different love languages? My daughter and I are completely different. I want to strengthen our

relationship by communicating in her language,
but I don't have that language. What do I do?

You will do your daughter a great service if you can understand and celebrate the ways she is different from you. *The
5 Love Languages*[2] is a great resource that can help you identify her love languages and learn what she needs from you.
For instance, if her love language is "words of affirmation"
but you never compliment her or affirm the good things she
does, you will miss opportunities to connect with her. You
say you don't have her language, but you can choose to speak
her language, even if it's not yours. Put away your assump-
tions of who you think she is and invite her to show you who
she really is. For further exploration, you may want to learn
about other ways of categorizing and understanding personality differences, such as the Myers-Briggs types, Kendall
Life Languages, or Enneagram. You could research on your
own or make it a fun family project. A good resource for
the Myers-Briggs types is *Please Understand Me*[3] by David
Keirsey.

acknowledgments

It's Momplicated would not have happened without our agent, Wendy Lawton of Books & Such Literary Management. Thank you, Wendy, for proposing the idea of a book about mothers and daughters. Writing this book has been a healing experience for both of us, and we want to express our sincere appreciation for your vision and your handling of this project. We also want to express our deep appreciation to the team at Tyndale. Jillian Schlossberg, you have been *our person.* Thank you for your insights and positivity. How serendipitous that we were birthing this book just as you were bringing your first daughter, Juliana, into the world! Sarah Atkinson, your vision and humor have inspired us; Kara Leonino, thank you for stepping in and keeping us going; Bonne Steffen, your editing has made this book a thousand times better; Julie Chen, thank you for the beautiful design; and Sharon Leavitt, your prayers and support have made all the difference. We know there are many others behind the scenes at Tyndale, and we appreciate each one of you.

I (Debbie) want to thank Joan for saying yes to partnering on this book. I thought that coauthoring would be hard, but with you it was seamless. We prayed, cried, laughed, did the happy dance, and somehow made it to the finish line loving each other more than when we started. The amount of healing I have received from our friendship and all that you brought to this project is beyond words. Joanie, I appreciate you so much!

Sue Boldt, I cannot acknowledge people without thanking you for the spiritual deposits you have made in my life. Sue, your friendship means more to me than you will ever know. Teresa Burke, Bettina Belter, and Christy Harper, your friendship over the years has been life-giving, and I thank God for you. The Wednesday night "Just-Sayin" sisters: Your support, prayers, and friendship mean so much to me, and I love doing life with you! Thank you to my ministry prayer team for praying me through this project for an entire year, from book proposal to finish. And a huge thanks to the Design4Living ministry team: Kendra Zierau, Kahlilah Guyah, and Janae Brier, your lives inspire me, and I love dreaming of equipping women with you.

A special thank-you to my family, who prayed for us as we wrote this book, often sending encouragement through our Alsdorf-Brier family texts. You all mean more to me than words can express.

Ashley and Megan, I am grateful that God merged our lives twenty-eight years ago, making me your stepmom. And though we have weathered blended-family momplications, we have also grown in love, friendship, and understanding. I love you and thank God for the gift of having you as daughters.

Janae and Kelly, I prayed for my sons' wives since they were little boys. You both represent God doing above and beyond anything I could have hoped for. Having a mother-in-law has its own momplications, and I thank God for your friendship and the grace you extend to me. You both are truly daughters to me, and I love you more as time goes on.

My precious first granddaughter, Jessa Lynn, you have been a catalyst for healing in Grammy's life as I worked on this book. Watching you, finding joy with you, and connecting with the little girl that you are helped me reconnect with the little girl in me. I love being your grammy. And my two newest granddaughters, Karis Elise and Lennox Joy, born as this book was being finished, I prayed while your mamas carried you and look forward to watching your lives unfold. I am blessed to be your grammy. I love you so much already.

Though this is a "girl" book, I have to mention my sons and grandsons. Justin and Cameron Brier, you have both brought immense joy to my life since the time you were born. Your friendship and love are such a gift, just as being your mother has been one of my life's greatest joys. I love you forever, like you for always . . . Easton, Pierce, McCartney, Declan, Jalen, and baby Cooper, each of you boys is loved and is so precious to your grammy (or GiGi; Easton, thank you for that special name). And sweet baby Jace Daniel, waiting for us in heaven, you will never be forgotten.

My sister, Sharon, you will always mean more to me than words can express. You were the one who held me as a baby, took me on outings with you and your teenage friends, and always made me feel special. I hope you know how much you are loved.

My mother, Irene Kenzie, you've been gone twenty years, but I still think of you every day. Thank you for the healing in our relationship, your honesty in the adult processing of our pain, and the joy of getting to understand each other more than ever in the end. Most especially, thank you for your very last words to me: "Live like it's real." I am reminded to live differently because of you, knowing this life isn't all there is. Our story is one of redemption. I love and miss you, Mama.

Saving the best for last, my sweet husband, Ray Alsdorf, it's impossible to thank you for everything you mean to me. You are my greatest support, my sweetest love, and the most precious gift. You have been a catalyst to my growth and healing, and I am forever grateful for you. I get to do what I do because of you. I love you more than the day we said, "I do."

I (Joan) first want to thank Debbie. Writing this book with you has truly been a joy. God has used you to encourage, heal, and stretch me beyond where I thought I could go. I am amazed at the opportunities he has given me through you. Your relationship with Christ inspires me, and I will be forever grateful for our friendship.

As we wrote this book about how God will meet our needs, I often thought of the many spiritual mothers and sisters he has brought to me. Elizabeth Brown, Diane Fox, and Karen Lahl, you were the most instrumental in my early spiritual life. Sally Beck, Monique Bell, Carrole Johnson, Deb Kleier Nakora, Diane Shore, and Kris Weaver, each of you has been immeasurably important to me. You have been there for me during the hard times, willing to listen and speak truth to me, sharing my passion for a life of intimacy with Christ. Lisa Shrewsbury, Judi Needham-Penrose, and Mary Jean Walton, you have been similarly dear friends, with the bonus that you are fellow therapists. Each of you has been a huge support and has helped me grapple with how God works through us to bring inner healing to others. Snowflakes—my kitchen table church—you have been with me weekly, encouraging me and praying for me at every stage of this book. Words cannot express the gratitude I feel that God has brought our little community into being. Thank you, Amy Closson, Janice Gutierrez, Diane Sims, Jill Vellinger, and Dianne Cantu, who I know is still praying for me from heaven.

Sara and Juli, my precious daughters, you have been an endless source of love and encouragement during this process. Thank you for being willing to honestly talk about our momplications, for always seeing the humor in things, and for being my biggest cheerleaders. D'Anne and Jennifer, you are my daughters in every way other than blood, and I love you more than I can say. Hilary and Madi, what a joy to be given two such lovely bonus daughters at this stage of my life. You are both treasures. Ellie Lien, I'm glad my sister's dream that you would be part of our family has been fulfilled. To my granddaughters—Karly, Baily, Alexa, and Maya—each of you is incredibly special to me, and I pray that I will leave a positive legacy in your lives.

Even though this is a "girl" book, I cannot overlook Sam, Carl, Kai, Jackson, and Dominic. My love and prayers are with you. To my future grandchildren and great-grandchildren, may hope and healing from this book flow down through the generations to bless you.

There has been a matriarchy of important women in my biological family, all of whom have passed away, but each of whom deserves acknowledgment and honor: my mother, Jane Dods Kniskern; my sister, Ann Kniskern; my grandmothers, Jane Wildman Dods and Vera Culver Kniskern; and my aunts, Betty Dods Lasek and Jean Kniskern Rawlins. Thank you all for the love and care you gave me. I miss each one of you.

I especially want to thank you, Mom. Through writing this book, I see more clearly than ever what a wonderful mother you were.

Steve Kay, my amazing husband, you have made me feel treasured and adored. Your faithful constancy is restoring my ability to trust. You have celebrated my every success and been a haven for me through every difficulty. You have helped me in very practical ways (love that chicken dish you make!) and have never complained about the long hours I put into this project. You are a kind, giving man who embodies the love of Christ to me. I'm grateful for you and I love you!

We both acknowledge that God has truly done more than we could have asked for or even imagined through *It's Momplicated*. We are amazed at his grace and favor. It is not easy to get a book published, but God threw the doors open for us and guided us through the entire process. He has used this book to grow us, and we are confident he will use it in the lives of others. He deserves all the glory.

notes

CHAPTER 2: EVERY WOMAN HAS AN IMPERFECT MOTHER

1. Daniel Seigel and Mary Hartzell, *Parenting from the Inside Out* (New York: Penguin Books, 2013), 173–212.
2. Peg Streep, "Daughters of Unloving Mothers: Mourning the Mom You Deserved," *Psychology Today* (blog), March 9, 2017, https://www.psychology today.com/blog/tech-support/201703/unloved-daughters-and-mourning -the-mother-you-deserved.
3. Ann Voskamp, *The Broken Way: A Daring Path into the Abundant Life* (Grand Rapids, MI: Zondervan, 2016).

CHAPTER 3: EVERY WOMAN CARRIES HER MOTHER'S MARK

1. Ruth Harms Calkin, *Lord, Could You Hurry a Little?* (Wheaton, IL: Tyndale House Publishers, 1983), 79.
2. Henri Nouwen, *Life of the Beloved* (New York: Crossroad, 2002), 32–33.
3. Mary D. Salter Ainsworth, Mary C. Blehar, Everett Waters, and Sally N. Wall, *Patterns of Attachment: A Psychological Study of the Strange Situation* (Hillsdale, NJ: Lawrence Erlbaum, 1978), 167; Mary Main and Judith Solomon, "Procedures for Identifying Infants as Disorganized/Disoriented during the Ainsworth Strange Situation," in *Attachment in the Preschool Years: Theory, Research, and Intervention*, ed. Mark T. Greenberg, Dante Cicchetti, and E. Mark Cummings (Chicago: University of Chicago Press, 1990), 121–60.

CHAPTER 4: EVERY WOMAN CAN LIVE A BETTER STORY

1. David Eckman, *Sex, Food, and God: The Struggle for the Heart* (BCWI Ministries, 2006), 123.

2. Avril Thorne, "Personal Memory Telling and Personality Development," *Personality and Social Psychology Review* 4, no. 1 (February 2000): 45–56.

CHAPTER 5: MOM, WHERE ARE YOU?

1. Margaret Wise Brown, *The Runaway Bunny* (New York: HarperCollins, 1972), 7.
2. Kelly McDaniel with Sarah Boggs, *Ready to Heal: Breaking Free of Addictive Relationships*, 3rd ed. (Carefree, AZ: Gentle Path Press, 2012), 173.

CHAPTER 6: MOM, WILL YOU KEEP ME SAFE?

1. "Joan Crawford's Daughter Christina Larry King Full Interview (2001)," YouTube video, from a televised episode of *Larry King Live* on August 10, 2001, posted by "TheConcludingChapterofCrawford," August 8, 2016, https://www.youtube.com/watch?v=2DxMIoks3SM.
2. Ibid.
3. Ibid.
4. Ibid.

CHAPTER 7: MOM, WILL YOU TEACH AND GUIDE ME?

1. Daniel Goleman, *Emotional Intelligence* (New York: Bantam Books, 1995).
2. Hope Edelman, *Motherless Daughters* (New York: Bantam, 1994).

CHAPTER 8: MOM, WILL YOU CELEBRATE ME AS A UNIQUE INDIVIDUAL?

1. Amy Chua, *Battle Hymn of the Tiger Mother* (London: Bloomsbury Publishing, 2011), 61–62.
2. Ibid, 3–5.
3. C. S. Lewis, *The Last Battle* (New York: HarperCollins, 2002), 206.

CHAPTER 9: HEALING STARTS WITH FACING REALITY

1. Mark Batterson, *The Circle Maker* (Grand Rapids, MI: Zondervan, 2011), 23.
2. Mark Batterson, *Draw the Circle: The 40 Day Prayer Challenge* (Grand Rapids: Zondervan, 2012), xx.
3. Batterson, *The Circle Maker*, 195.

CHAPTER 10: HEALING CONTINUES BY LIVING IN THE TRUTH

1. Tim Hansel, *You Gotta Keep Dancin'* (Colorado Springs: David C Cook Publishing, 1998), 124.
2. Sandra Wilson, "The Sufficiency of Christ in Counseling," speech given at the annual conference of the American Association of Christian Counseling, Philadelphia, March 1995.

3. Neil T. Anderson and Robert L. Saucy, *The Common Made Holy* (Eugene, OR: Harvest House, 1997), 191.

4. Sue Boldt, *Steps to Breakthrough: Freedom from Life's Hurts Workbook* (self-pub., CreateSpace, 2016).

5. A. W. Tozer, *Gems from Tozer* (Camp Hill, PA: Christian Publications, 1979), 35.

CHAPTER 11: HEALING CAN HAPPEN IN YOUR CURRENT RELATIONSHIP

1. Credit for the idea of using the Serenity Prayer in this way goes to Mary Anne Fifield, PhD, *The Serenity Prayer: Making It Personal* (self-published, 2013).

CHAPTER 12: CHANGING THE LEGACY YOU LEAVE

1. Sally Clarkson, *Own Your Life* (Carol Stream, IL: Tyndale, 2014), 225.

2. Neil T. Anderson and Robert L. Saucy, *The Common Made Holy* (Eugene, OR: Harvest House, 1997), 16.

3. Adapted from Debbie Alsdorf, *Deeper: Living in the Reality of God's Love* (Grand Rapids, MI: Revell, 2008), 18–22.

Q&A WITH DEBBIE AND JOAN . . .

1. An excellent and readable resource for building your listening skills is *I Don't Have to Make Everything All Better* by Gary and Joy Lundberg.

2. Gary Chapman, *The 5 Love Languages* (Chicago: Northfield Publishing, 2015).

3. David Keirsey, *Please Understand Me II: Temperament, Character, Intelligence* (Del Mar, CA: Prometheus Nemesis Book Company, 1998).

about the authors

Author and international speaker **DEBBIE ALSDORF**'s mission is to help women live a better story by leading them to the heart of God's love and the truth of his Word. She has spent the majority of her adult life involved in women's ministries as well as being a biblical lay counselor and Christian life coach. In 2005, she brought together a team and founded Design4Living Ministries to challenge women to experience spiritual transformation, equipping women for a life of faith. Debbie has authored Bible studies, books, and curriculums. In addition, she has been a featured writer for Calvary Chapel, In Touch, and Focus on the Family. Debbie and her husband, Ray, have raised a blended family of four adult children. Today Debbie's favorite role is being a grandma to ten little ones.

JOAN EDWARDS KAY is a licensed marriage and family therapist with a private practice in the East Bay of San Francisco. Her mission is to help individuals and couples find freedom from old, painful beliefs and patterns so they can experience joyful connection with themselves, others, and God. Joan has been an adjunct professor at Western Seminary and has taught classes on various counseling topics at churches in her area. She is a member of the California Association of Marriage and Family Therapists and the American Association of Christian Counselors. Joan received her bachelor's degree from Vassar College and her master's degree from Western Seminary. Joan is happily married and has two adult daughters, four stepdaughters, and five grandchildren.

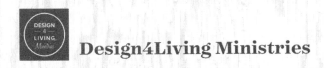

Design4Living Ministries

Design4Living is a nonprofit 501(c)(3) ministry committed to equipping women for lives of faith. Debbie Alsdorf, the cofounder and president of Design4Living, leads a team of dedicated women providing events and resources for discipleship, mentoring, and spiritual growth. Design4Living will be expanding in the future with teams to additionally reach men and married couples.

Values
4 ways to love God (Mark 12:30)
Heart ᚥ Soul ᚥ Mind ᚥ Strength

Beliefs
4 truths to build stability and peace (Psalm 139)
He knows me ᚥ He protects me
He created me ᚥ He values me

Mission
4 truths that simplify life's mission
(Colossians 1:16; Matthew 22:37-40)
I have been created by God ᚥ I have been created for God
I have been created to love God
I have been created to love others

To follow the ministry blog, visit www.design4living.org.

For information on seminars, retreats, and events, e-mail
admin@design4living.org.

To follow Debbie's *Living Up!* blog, visit www.debbiealsdorf.com.

CP1412